Finding Out About

LIFE IN BRITAIN IN THE 1960s

Nigel Richardson

B.T. Batsford Limited, *London*

Contents

Typeset by Tek-Art Ltd, Kent
and printed and bound in Great Britain
by Richard Clay Ltd,
Chichester, Sussex
for the publishers
B.T. Batsford Limited,
4 Fitzhardinge Street
London W1H 0AH

ISBN 0 7134 4816 4

ACKNOWLEDGMENTS

The Author and Publishers thank the following for their permission to reproduce the illustrations: Catholic Pictorial, page 14; Daily Telegraph, page 35 (right); Family Planning Association, page 8; Leicester Mercury, pages 17, 32; Northern Songs Ltd, page 29; The Photo Source, front cover (bottom left), frontispiece, pages 9, 12, 23 (top), 30, 35 (left), 39; Private Eye, pages 18, 26, 27; Punch, pages 7, 21, 23 (bottom), 37; Shelter, page 15; Simplicity Patterns Ltd, front cover, top; Tate Gallery, page 19 (© DACS 1985), page 19. The photographs on pages 3, 4, 20, 40, 41 are from the Author's collection. The maps on pages 33 and 44 were drawn by R.F. Brien. Thanks are also due to all the printed sources mentioned in the book.

Frontispiece: Concorde 002, *on show for the first time at Filton, Bristol, 1968.*

People nowadays look at the 1960s in two contrasting ways. In one way the decade is seen as a time of great excitement — a time whose passing we regret and a time when change was always in the air. Britain seemed to have far fewer problems than she has now; unemployment and oil prices were still very low. The British people were discovering new experiences like the music of The Beatles, foreign holidays and exciting new fashions. It was a time of optimism and hope; people really did believe that they were helping to create a better world and that economic prosperity would continue to grow for ever.

On the other hand, people also look back on the Sixties with amusement and even contempt. The demands of student protestors and hippies seem rather ridiculous to many people now — we are much more inclined nowadays to think that the world could never get by on a diet of flowers, peace and love, and protest in that way looks like a luxury that we can no longer afford. Many of the hippies of the Sixties have become the pin-striped executives of the Eighties. We are a much more serious generation than the Sixties was — where Sixties' people were all for pulling down

old traditions merely because they had existed for a long time, we have become much more wary of change for change's sake. We are also much more aware of Britain's declining position in the world and of the length of the dole queues — especially in the North.

What is certain, though, is that a spirit of CHANGE was everywhere in the 1960s. You can see aspects of it on nearly every page of this book, from Britain's changing role in the world to the changes in everyday surroundings in home, school and office. Organizations like the Church, the Scouts and the universities had to come to terms with dramatically changing attitudes amongst young people; those working in architecture and the arts had to accept new materials and styles. The entertainment industry had to come to terms with the threat that television posed to radio, the cinema and newspapers. The theatre had to adjust to the end of dramatic

People can change a great deal in ten years — especially if they are growing up then. The first photograph shows the author (on the left) and his two brothers on holiday in 1960. The second shows the author, also on holiday, in 1970.

censorship. Government had to accept the need for changes in transport patterns, the police had to fight increasingly expert criminals, and politicians had to wrestle with the new problems caused by pollution, nationalism in Scotland and Wales and terrorism in Northern Ireland. People had to come to terms with a host of new things, from weather reports in centigrade as well as fahrenheit, to Premium Bonds, Bingo and the Duke of Edinburgh's Award Scheme. Those working in many professions had to begin to come to terms with computers.

Meanwhile the decade saw a series of momentous events abroad. The Sixties began with an icy "Cold War" between America and Russia, made colder still in 1961-2 by events in Berlin and Cuba. A new, youthful, American President, John F. Kennedy, took the world by storm in 1961, only to be cruelly assassinated after less than three years in office. As the decade continued there was civil war in Africa, crisis in the Middle East, the Russian invasion of Czechoslovakia and the landing of the first man on the Moon. All through the decade events in Vietnam cast a terrible shadow, not only over the United States but also over much of the Western world – and eventually exploded into riots across America and Europe.

Anyone trying to compile a book about the Sixties has one great problem – what to leave out. There is so much that could be included, so much that could be recorded in more detail. Maybe those who have compiled other books in this series would say the same about their own periods of history. But the "Swinging Sixties" was a very special time. Those of us who grew up in it were dimly aware of the fact at the time. Looking back now, we know it for certain.

1. PEOPLE

a) There are still a great many people alive who remember the 1960s well. Those who are now aged 35-40 will be able to tell you a lot about what it was like to be a teenager then; those of 60 or so may well remember how difficult it was to decide what to allow their children to do and what to stop them doing at a time when so many new ideas and attitudes were sweeping through society. Your parents, relatives and teachers will all have their own memories.

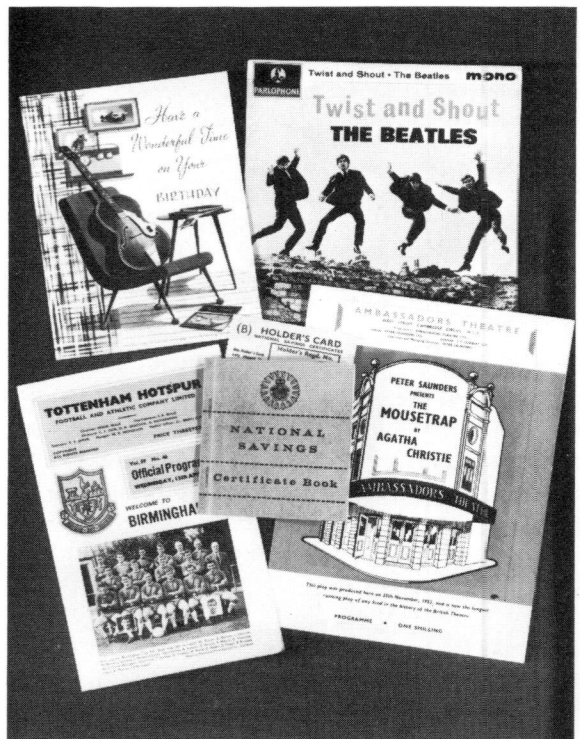

See if you can find old 1960s' magazines, theatre programmes, election pamphlets, household bills . . .

Ask your parents and friends to look for documents, scrapbooks, record sleeves and boxes of little things which people keep because they somehow cannot bear to throw them away! Attics and wardrobes or cupboards may also reveal 1960s' clothes and documents which have been forgotten about long ago.

2. PLACES TO VISIT

a) *Buildings* A great deal of adventurous new building took place in the Sixties, especially in concrete. Walk round the centre of your nearest town or city and see how much of it you can discover Shopping centres and office blocks may well date from that time. Can you find out what was there before? Were the new buildings an improvement?

b) *Museums* An increasing number of museums – for example, the Museum of London – are devoting space to exhibits which were in use by ordinary people only a few years ago.

3. VISUAL SOURCES

a) *Maps and photographs* Many public libraries have special sections for maps and for books of photographs. The Ordnance Survey maps (6" and 25" scale) are especially helpful. Ask the librarian if there are maps of the same area from the 1960s and from before. Comparing these, you will be able to see what changes occurred in the 1960s. How is the same area different today? See if you can find annual collections of photographs published in the Sixties. They may well be in a shelf of outsize books. Many families also have albums or boxes of school and wedding photographs which can tell you a great deal about Sixties' styles.

b) *Films* There are still plenty of 1960s' films shown on TV. See what you can learn about fashions hair-styles, language, furniture, etc.

4. WRITTEN SOURCES

a) *Books* There is a short book list on page 47. See how many of the books you can find in your library and ask the librarian if she or he knows of any others about life in the 1960s.

b) *Newspapers and magazines* Most larger libraries keep back numbers of national newspapers or have had their papers copied on to microfilm. Study the advertisements as well as the news stories – you can learn a great deal from them. Local newspapers are especially useful for their advertisements. Magazines like *Punch* and *Private Eye* have useful photographs and cartoons. Look out for old copies of *Radio Times* and of magazines like *Honey*. You may find old 1960s' newspapers being used to line drawers in houses where people have lived for a long time.

School magazines and parish magazines are also very useful and many libraries have copies of these.

c) *Hansard* This detailed record of parliamentary debates is available in large libraries.

d) *Keesings Contemporary Archives* Sometimes these are quite difficult to understand, but they provide a good summary of world events, especially if you use the index carefully. The Archives are added to each month, and are available in many libraries.

e) *Local council minutes* These can often tell you a lot about the important local issues of the day. The local reference library may be able to help you to find these and other useful documents.

You've Never Had It So Good!

This slogan was an election-winner for Prime Minister Harold Macmillan in 1959. In many ways, it was quite true; towards the end of the 1950s Britain finally shook off the economic hardships caused by the 1939-45 war, and the 1960s was an optimistic time. The British enjoyed an economic "Boom" — wages rose faster than prices. Between 1960 and 1970 the number of private cars doubled from 5.6m to 11.8m. In 1961, nearly all manual workers had only two weeks' holiday a year; ten years later, 99% of them had at least three weeks, and 50% had four or more. Suddenly the shops were full of a huge variety of goods at prices which people could afford. Life seemed good, and everyone assumed that this was bound to last.

But "Boom" also brought inflation — a rapid rise in prices — in the late 1960s. Prices rose partly because of the increased demands for goods, and partly because British industry was becoming out of date, especially compared with countries like West Germany which had rebuilt factories completely after the war. The Government had to draw up an "incomes policy" — to "freeze" prices and wages at fixed levels for a time, so that Britain would still be able to sell goods abroad at prices which foreigners would be prepared to pay. This policy was fiercely resisted by the Trade Unions.

EATING OUT

> **Suddenly there was an amazing variety of food in restaurants. Not many people travelled abroad before 1960, and you could usually order only one type of pasta. But by 1970, Italian, Indian and Chinese food was everywhere.** (Roy Collard, born 1952)

Can you think of any other reason why it suddenly became possible to buy so many more foreign foods in the 1960s? Which technological improvements would have helped this?

IT'S ON! A FIGHT TO THE FINISH

This was a *Daily Mail* headline in 1966.

> **Britain's first Merchant Navy stoppage since 1911 starts tomorrow. The strike is the biggest industrial showdown since Mr. George Brown, the TUC and the employers drew up the incomes policy eighteen months ago. The seamen have more industrial power than almost any other group of workers and believe they are in a strong bargaining position.** (*Daily Mail*, 14 May 1966)

> **Wholesale prices of meat, fruit and vegetables rocketed by up to 60% within hours of the start of the Seamen's Strike.** (*Daily Mail*, 17 May 1966)

Can you work out why the prices of these goods should have risen so soon after the strike began?

DEVALUING THE POUND

In 1967 the Government decided to devalue the pound — to cut its value compared with the dollar and with the currencies of other countries — by 14%. This would stop the price of British cars and other goods sold abroad from getting much higher than those of foreign producers.

> **There had been devaluation rumours for weeks. When it came one of my friends was very pleased. He had changed £100 into dollars the previous day, and when he changed the money back on Monday he would get £114. But most people gradually realized that devaluation was a sign of Britain's declining place in the world. The 1970s were to prove this.** (Nigel Richardson, a student in 1967)

"Threepennyworth of pepper? Third left, second right, left-hand side, third shelf down, fourth compartment from the left and the basket's to help you carry it."

Can you find any extract on this page which has the same message as this cartoon from Punch (19 January 1966)?

INFLATION: A PERSONAL MEMORY

My grandmother was elderly and unable to go out of the house for much of the 1960s. Every birthday and Christmas I received the same thing – a £1 note. I tried always to sound both surprised and grateful. In 1960, £1 seemed a lot of money to me, and I looked after it very carefully while I decided all the things to spend it on. By 1970, £1 was worth much less – it would buy me one course of a meal in a very ordinary restaurant. (Peter Vincent, born 1948)

Can you discover a restaurant advertisement in a 1960s' copy of your local paper? Does it give any of the meal prices? If not, see if you can discover whether the restaurant still exists, and whether the people who work there still have a 1960s' menu or price list. How do the prices compare with the prices now?

From 1940 to 1970 Britain's population grew from about 47m to over 55m. This was due partly to higher standards of living, but also to notable advances in medicine. In the 1960s medical breakthroughs were gradually enabling doctors to save more lives than ever before. The contraceptive pill was available, to help people control the number of children they decided to have. The 1967 Abortion Act allowed doctors to end a pregnancy by surgical methods to avoid damage to the health of the mother, or if the baby seemed likely to be handicapped in some way.

There was an old woman who lived in a shoe She had so many children she didn't know what to do

She had never heard of Family Planning

Your nearest FPA clinic is

THE WORLD'S FIRST HUMAN HEART TRANSPLANT

In December 1967 Professor Christiaan Barnard of South Africa carried out the world's first human heart transplant. The donor was a young woman who had been killed in a motor accident. The man who received the heart, Louis Washkansky, died after 18 days of pneumonia, although the operation was a surgical success.

> We were ready to place the heart in its future home. Gently Rodney lifted it into the empty chest of Washkansky. For a moment I stared at it, wondering how it would ever work. It seemed so small and insignificant – too tiny to ever handle all the demands that would be put upon it.

THE POPE SPEAKS OUT AGAINST BIRTH CONTROL

> Pope Paul yesterday delivered his long-awaited ruling on birth control – and brought disappointment and despair to many of the world's hundred million Roman Catholics. In a 38-page encyclical letter "Of human life" he declared that the Pill, all male and female contraceptives, sterilisation and abortion are sinful, and he called on leaders of the world's governments to outlaw them as a means of limiting the population. (*The Sun*, 30 July 1968)

What is the Roman Catholic Church's present teaching about birth control? Can you find out why it holds this view? Do you agree with it?

◁ *A poster produced by the Family Planning Association in the 1960s. What exactly do you think this poster is trying to say?*

Then we began the first step, which was to sew the two openings in the top of the donor heart onto the two valves of the waiting lid. . . .

Ozzie switched on a 20-joule charge of TK volts. It shot through the squirming muscles, causing the body of Louis Washkansky to arch upwards as though kicked in the back. For a moment the heart lay paralysed, without any sign of life. We waited – it seemed like hours – until it slowly began to relax. Then it came, like a bolt of light. . . . Little by little [the heart] began to roll with the lovely rhythm of life, the heart-beat of the world. . . .
(*One Life* by Christiaan Barnard, Harrap, 1970)

A number of parents of Thalidomide children took the drug manufacturers to court in an attempt to make them pay compensation. Here Mr Justice Hinchcliffe visits a Thalidomide child before deciding the amount that should be paid.

THALIDOMIDE

All new medical techniques and new drugs need lengthy research and involve some risks. In 1960 and 1961 a number of children were born with deformed arms and legs, or without them altogether. The cause was traced to a new drug called Thalidomide.

Fair-haired Neil Carter faces 1968, and his first full year at School, with all the bounce and energy of any 5-year old. But Neil has no arms.

Neil was born five years ago when Thalidomide was still being prescribed to expectant mothers. "Can I show the man my Christmas present?", he asked his mother at the Carter home. Then, using his feet with a delicate artistry, played with the timing controls of a mechanical bull-dozer in easy fashion.

His mother, Mrs. Joyce Carter explained – "He sometimes amazes us with the things he can do. He writes, paints, feeds himself and he has now started dressing himself." Neil, a victim of science, is now being helped by technology. He is already getting power-assisted artificial arms for a short spell. . . . (*Leicester Mercury*, 1 January 1968)

What medical discovery would you most like to see made in the 1980s?

Science and Technology

The 1960s was a period of notable scientific progress and a time when politicians had a great deal to say about its importance. Harold Wilson, leader of the Labour Party, told the Party Conference in 1963:

> **First, we must produce more scientists. Secondly, having produced them here, we must be a great deal more successful in keeping them in this country. Thirdly, having trained them, we must make more intelligent use of them. . . . Fourthly, we must organise British industry so that it applies the results of scientific research more purposively to our national production effort.**

What do you notice when you compare this report from 1961 of the first man in space with the report of the moon landing in 1969?
▽

The British Petroleum giant has stepped on the North Sea Gas at just the right moment. . . . Not that the new-found wealth is round the corner. "It's only a whiff, we wish it was more," says the BP Chairman. The hope is that the whiff will become something economically more substantial. . . .
(*The Observer*, 26 September 1965)

The leading favourite in the race to find natural gas beneath the sea rises out of the grey water like a ten-legged monster.

   Already British Petroleum's 250 ft long drilling platform has made the strike that the Minister of Power, Mr. Fred Lee called "probably the most exciting happening in Britain today".
(*The Observer*, 19 December 1965)

Why do you think Mr Lee thought it was all so exciting?

In 1967 the decision was taken to develop the *Concorde* aircraft as a joint Anglo-French project. The aircraft was designed to transport passengers faster than the speed of sound.

The maiden flight of Concorde took place at Toulouse on March 2nd [1969]. The aircraft took off at 3.30 pm and flew for 27 minutes, reaching an altitude of 10,000 ft, but not exceeding 300 miles an hour in speed. After one practice

THE Q.E.2

The Queen launched the ship at Clydebank and named it Queen Elizabeth II. For a full minute after the launching button was pressed, the new queen of the seas appeared not to move . . . then the liner, her personality imprinted on the cheering thousands, moved swiftly and gracefully down to the water, where tugs manoeuvred her towards the fitting-out berth. . . . The ship will go as fast as the earlier queens on half the fuel consumption, and this will save still more space to be used for more and better passenger cabins. (*Illustrated London News*, 30 September 1967)

THE MOON LANDING: A PERSONAL RECOLLECTION

I watched TV pictures of Neil Armstrong's moon landing while I was having breakfast in a hotel in Rome. Everyone in the dining room was glued to the set, hardly noticing what they were eating; the waiters kept bringing things and then stopping for a long time to watch. Outside there was far less traffic than on a normal day, as everyone stayed at home to watch, or went to work early to watch in the office. We were also shown frequent pictures of the Pope having breakfast as *he* watched the landing. (Elizabeth Davies, a student in 1969)

Can you find anyone who remembers where he or she saw this event?

MAN CONQUERED THE MOON TODAY BEFORE A WATCHING TELEVISION AUDIENCE OF 500 MILLION

And as America's new frontiersman Neil Armstrong planted his foot firmly on the grey, lunar desert he said, in a slightly shaking voice:

"That's one small step for a man . . . but one giant leap for mankind.". . .

Back on earth, President Nixon picked up a telephone and in a history-making link-up call he told the intrepid pioneers: "As you talk to us from the Sea of Tranquillity it inspires us to redouble our efforts to bring peace and tranquillity to earth.

"For one priceless moment in the whole history of man all the people on this earth are truly one: one in their pride in what you have done and one in our prayers that you will return safely to earth."

The return is scheduled for 6.55 London time tonight, after what America's space chiefs say is "the greatest thing since man started making machines and exploring". Meanwhile the astronauts are sleeping. (*London Evening Standard*, 21 July 1969)

approach at high altitude the aircraft landed. Second and third test flights were made on March 9th and 13th lasting for 61 and 49 minutes respectively. (*Keesings Contemporary Archives*)

What can you find out about the role of *Concorde* in the 1980s?

Pollution

The 1960s was the decade when people began to see the threats to their surroundings from noise, dirt and chemical poisoning. At the end of the Sixties some people also began to point out that the world's resources might one day run out unless they were carefully conserved, although this did not become a major public concern until the Seventies.

A gale pounds the Torrey Canyon, *29 March 1367.*

NOISE POLLUTION

During the 1960s the Government decided to build London's third airport at Stansted in Essex. This provoked a huge outcry in the surrounding area.

> **A letter asking the Prime Minister to intervene to save Thaxted Parish Church, Essex from damage by aircraft vibration if Stansted becomes London's third airport was handed to Mr. Wilson on Saturday by Lord Butler, Master of Trinity College, Cambridge.**
>
> **The proposed main runway of the new airport will pass directly over the 181 ft high spire and villagers fear that vibrations caused by large aeroplanes will cause it to collapse.** (*Church Times*, 20 May 1967)

What has happened to Stansted since then?

THE THREAT FROM LITTER: A RECOLLECTION

The increasing use of throw-away, non-returnable containers, often made from materials which would not dissolve or rot of their own accord, began to cause pollution problems, too.

> **In July 1969 I crossed the English Channel by ferry. As I looked over the side a hatch suddenly opened below me and two cardboard boxes were thrown out of the kitchens on the deck below. A trail of plastic cups, tins and paper wrappers drifted across the water. I remembered the last beach I had walked along and what I had found there. Suddenly I understood what 'Pollution' meant.** (Nigel Richardson, born 1948)

What do you think the author meant when he said he "remembered the last beach he had walked along"?

THE TORREY CANYON

In the spring of 1967, the Liberian oil tanker *Torrey Canyon* ran aground on rocks off Land's End, and broke her back.

The Torrey Canyon – aground on the Seven Stones Reef for 8 days – was destroyed in a bombing raid by Royal Navy Buccaneers on March 28th. The jets had flown direct from Lossiemouth, Scotland, by order of the Home Secretary, Mr. Roy Jenkins. A 2,000 ft pall of smoke rose over the tanker which earlier had split into three – releasing another 30,000 tons of oil. About 10,000 tons had already contaminated an 80-mile stretch of the Cornish coast. . . . (*Illustrated London News*, 1 April 1967)

Two weeks after the Torrey Canyon ran aground, we went on holiday in North Devon. Although we were miles from the Seven Stones Reef, the remains of the Torrey Canyon's cargo could be seen all around us as soon as we went down to the water's edge – lots and lots of tiny little globules of oil, being gently washed in by the tide. When we scraped the surface sand off the beach, we found plenty more, and when we got back to the car our shoes were covered with oil. (Christopher Trillo, aged 15 in 1967)

Can you find out the main methods used to deal with oil pollution on beaches?

SMOKELESS ZONES AGAINST SMOG

To restrict air pollution in cities, 1960s' governments insisted that many householders use only smokeless fuel in their grates. Smokeless zones were introduced in many cities; gradually, "smog", common before the early 1960s, became a thing of the past.

Twenty-eight deaths attributable to smog occurred in the London area yesterday, making 60 since Monday, December 3. Health authorities made emergency plans for treating smog victims.

Fog again covered much of the country and the Automobile Association said that it was the worst for 10 years. Traffic in parts of London was brought to a stand-still during the afternoon.

The 28 deaths in London yesterday were of people aged between 37 and 86 and comprised 19 men and nine women. Twenty collapsed indoors, six in the street and two at work.

The amount of smoke in the London air was 10 times higher than normal for a winter day yesterday. The amount of sulphur dioxide was 14 times higher than normal. (*Daily Telegraph*, 6 December 1962)

From what you have just read, can you work out exactly what "smog" was?

Buildings and Housing

Viewed from the air, the cities of the 1960s showed great contrasts. Exciting new ideas about building design and the discovery of new ways of using building materials, such as concrete and glass, led to some striking pieces of architecture. The Cambridge University History Library is one; the Roman Catholic Cathedral in Liverpool is another. However, there were still a large number of elderly, "slum" housing areas in the 1960s. The Government and the local councils made great efforts in the Sixties to build new homes – 413,700 were built in 1968, far more than in single years in the 1970s. But it was not enough; many people remained in great poverty or had no home at all. And many of the new homes were in tower-blocks of flats, which caused new problems.

One of the most adventurous pieces of 1960s' architecture was the Roman Catholic Cathedral in Liverpool. An architects' competition was held: no design was allowed to cost more than £1m at 1959 prices. Eighty architects entered. Sir Frederick Gibberd won the £5,000 prize. Some people said the Cathedral, with its glass dome representing Jesus' crown of thorns, was a masterpiece; others nicknamed it "Paddy's Wigwam" and "The Mersey Funnel".

SHELTER

Bad housing is responsible for much social evil. That is the belief of the Reverend Bruce Kenrick, the initiator and chairman of Shelter – a national campaign for the homeless to be launched in London on December 1st. The money it raises will go towards providing accommodation where the situation is worst: London, Glasgow, Birmingham, and Liverpool. Funds will be channelled direct to efficient housing associations in these cities.

Three million families in Britain today live in slums, near slums or in overcrowded conditions. . . . The strain imposed on a family washing, dressing, eating, sleeping, and playing in one room may lead to it breaking up and to crime and juvenile delinquency. (Adam Lynford, *Illustrated London News*, 3 December 1966)

CATHY COME HOME

In 1966 a BBC television play about the housing crisis was seen by a huge audience. It was called *Cathy Come Home*, and did a great deal to publicize the problem of those with nowhere to go. Des Wilson, who was Director of Shelter and a fierce critic of the Government for not doing enough about the homeless, talked about the play:

For over an hour Britain was captured by Cathy – Cathy hitch-hiking to London, Cathy meeting and marrying a delivery driver, Cathy having a baby, Cathy's husband getting badly hurt jumping from his skidding lorry, Cathy's family moving into a squalid

NEW HOMES IN GLASGOW

A 1967 Government report found that one person in three in Scotland lived in a home considered to be sub-standard. Glasgow's slums were widely thought to be the worst in Europe. But although Glasgow made great efforts to improve things, the new blocks of flats produced new problems of their own.

Shelter is an organization founded in the 1960s to publicize conditions in poor city areas. As this Shelter poster shows, life in tower blocks was not as attractive as the planners hoped it would be. Many residents found their homes lonely and isolated.

... Glasgow has built the tallest residential flats, a soaring 31-storey block 300 feet high at Balornock's Red Road site. At a cost of £6¼m the Corporation have built 1350 houses, 73 lock-ups and 252 car spaces – "birdcage room" for 4500 people. These towering blocks, like many others in the city, would almost seem designed to be the monumental slums of the twenty-first century. Glasgow's sky-scrapers are littered with notices banning children from playing; the lifts small, inadequate, and often do not work. ... Loneliness is intensified by the fact that mothers dare not let their three- or four-year-olds downstairs unaccompanied. Children, when they first go to school, are sometimes withdrawn. They do not fit in; the seeds of isolation and mental trouble have already been sown. (Arthur Foster, *Illustrated London News*, 9 December 1967)

tenement, then a derelict caravan site, then a hostel for the homeless, then Cathy being evicted, and finally Cathy's family breaking up.

Jeremy Sandford (the author of the play) wrote:

"And then Cathy was filled with some fund of energy that she hadn't known about. She was like an animal now, as she fought to keep her children. And they overpowered Cathy and held her down and the children were carried off. Cathy screamed, yelled and then her sobs subsided. She was left moaning to herself.

A passer-by asked Cathy was she all right and she said she was all right.

She rose from the seat and went to the 'all-nite T Bar' and spent her last fourpence on a cup of tea.

She had one penny left."

Britain was indignant. If this gaping hole in the welfare state couldn't be kept decently under the carpet then someone somewhere had to be blamed. So the Labour Party blamed ... the thirteen years of Conservative administration, and the Conservatives blamed ... socialist-controlled councils. (From *I Know It Was the Place's Fault*, by Des Wilson, Oliphant, 1970)

The 1960s was a period of great changes in schools. Language laboratories, record players, tape recorders and television sets began to appear. Project work became fashionable. In the 1950s most secondary-age children attended either a grammar school, if they had passed an exam at 11+, or a secondary modern school if they had not. But by the 1960s many people, including Labour Party politicians, had come to believe that selection at 11 was much too early. They favoured comprehensive schools, which would include all the children in an area whatever their academic ability, and which tended, therefore, to have very large numbers of pupils. Opponents of comprehensive schools said that they would fail to allow really clever children to develop their full abilities. In 1965 the Labour Government ordered local education authorities to draw up plans for comprehensive education.

Other new ideas included taking girls into boys' public school sixth forms and a growing doubt about the use of corporal punishment. The CSE exam was introduced in 1965; many of the exams were set by the teachers themselves. Generally, there was much more questioning of those in authority, rather than merely doing what you were told. Older pupils were much less ready to control younger ones.

COMPREHENSIVE SCHOOLS: FOR AND AGAINST

The arguments against our divided system of education mount higher day by day. Parents are no longer content to accept the verdict of mental tests at 11. . . . In exam results, comprehensive schools are already turning the tables on those who raised alarm about the threat to academic standards. . . . (From *The Comprehensive School* by Robin Pedley, Penguin Books, 1963)

If this policy goes through there will never again exist in Britain schools for the cleverer sons of railwaymen or miners. . . . We shall be lowering standards where they matter most to the country's competitive efficiency. (*The Times Educational Supplement*, 14 May 1965)

MEMORIES OF A COMPREHENSIVE SCHOOL

Living on Clifton Estate, near Nottingham, Steve and I went to the same boys' school – Fairham School, a new comprehensive for 1,800 boys. It was very different for the girls, though. One of Steve's sisters went to the Secondary school, the other to the Bilateral school and my sister went to the Grammar school. They all had different groups of friends. At Fairham Steve and I were in the same house and the same tutor group – John Hunt house, group F (Hf). There were eight houses, each with eight tutor groups of about five boys from each year group. We were in different forms, though, because classes were streamed but at break and lunch times we'd swap stories, compare homeworks and play football – sometimes with my class mates, other times with his. After school we'd go to the hobbies' clubs and team practices and then in the evenings we'd all meet up again at one of the many youth clubs in Clifton. After taking CSEs Steve left school to work

A revolutionary design in school building –
Countesthorpe, Leicestershire.

"ANGRY YOUNG MEN"

This phrase was first used to describe a group of 1950s' playwrights who challenged traditional opinions and ideas. By the mid-1960s the challenge had become much more widespread. One man who experienced many of the new ideas of 1960s' teenagers at first hand was a housemaster in a boarding school from 1955 until 1970, responsible for 55 boys aged 13-18:

In 1955 things were not all that different from the 1930s when I was at school myself. But by 1970 the boys questioned

many more things. Once, when they had been told that things were done in a certain way in the past and that this was the proper way to do them, they had accepted it. But by the mid-1960s, after the arrival of The Beatles, they began to say that if that was the way things had been done for so many years, then it was time for a change. Tradition began to have a bad meaning, and experimenting with new ideas and methods was what mattered.

It was more difficult to arouse enthusiasm or a sense of patriotism. Perhaps the greatest change of all came in religion. In 1955 it was fairly easy to teach the main beliefs of the Church. By 1970 it was much more difficult to convince boys about the old religious truths which had once been accepted without doubt. (Bryan Matthews, a public school master from 1941-77)

as an apprentice electrician but we still met with everyone at the youth club.
(Gary Cooke, born 1956)

In what ways does Fairham School sound similar to or different from the one you go to?

Why do you think the arrival of The Beatles was thought to be so important?

The Permissive Society

The 1960s was a decade when ideas, language and actions which had previously been thought to be wrong suddenly became acceptable. "Freedom" was a demand on many people's lips; those who disapproved of it spoke of a new "Permissive Society" – one which would permit anything.

Two distinct youth groups, very different in style and interests, were known as Mods and Rockers. Violent fights took place between them during Bank Holiday weekends in 1964 at several coastal towns including Bournemouth, Hastings and Brighton. The newspapers blamed boredom and a determination by young people to challenge the authorities, especially the police.

MODS . . .

The leaders of mod fashion tended to buy their outfits in the newly opened boutiques of Carnaby Street. . . . It was a busy life. A mod called Denzil, interviewed in the Sunday Times magazine in 1964 described an 'average' week. On Monday night he would go dancing at the Mecca, the Hammersmith Palais, the Purley Orchid or the Streatham Locarno. On Tuesday night he would be at the Scene Club in Soho. Wednesday was Marquee night, while Thursday was set aside for hair-washing. On Friday he would be back at the Scene Club. Saturday afternoon was spent shopping for clothes and records; after that he would go out dancing and would rarely return before 9 o'clock on Sunday morning. On Sunday evening he would go to the Flamingo – or he might get an early night. (From *The Sixties* by Francis Wheen, Century Publishing/Channel 4, 1982)

. . . AND ROCKERS

If there's one thing that I like, it's a
  burn-up on my bike
A burn-up with a bird up on my bike.
Now the M1 ain't much fun 'til you try
  and do a ton
A burn-up with a bird up on my bike.
Just for kicks I ride all through the
  night;
My bird hangs on in fright when I do the
  ton for kicks.
We meet the other ton-up boys at Fred's
  cafe every night
We just drops in to see the birds and
  sometimes have a bite
We spends a couple of hours just tuning
  our machines
With our black and leather jackets and
  our oily, greasy jeans. . . . ("Just for
Kicks", Mike Sarne, Parlophone Records,
1964)

What do you think were the main differences between Mods and Rockers?

Two clergymen supposedly discussing the effects of the Permissive Society. (Private Eye)

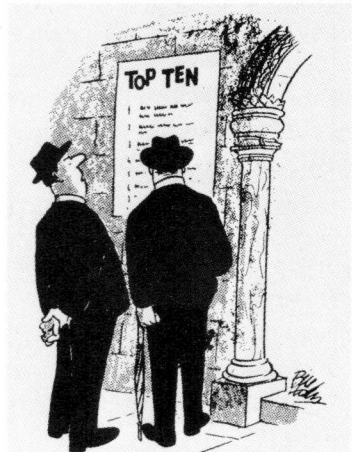

"I see 'Thou shalt not commit adultery''s dropped to eighth . . ."

MARY WHITEHOUSE

Older people were not slow to condemn what they saw as the worst results of permissiveness. Mary Whitehouse launched a national campaign against sex and violence on television and became one of the leading critics of the Permissive Society.

Mrs. Mary Whitehouse, a schoolteacher, has launched a national campaign to help writers who find it difficult to induce BBC TV to screen their work. She said yesterday – "Authors who speak out strongly for the established Christian faith and write plays which inspire a sense of purpose and hope find it extraordinarily difficult to get their work accepted."

Mrs. Whitehouse, 53, is founder of the Women of Britain Clean up TV Campaign. She added "It became necessary because of the built-in censorship which the BBC exerts against much that is good and clean in our national culture". (*Daily Mail*, 25 May 1964)

Do you think there should be any restriction on what is shown in the cinema or on TV? Is there any difference between the two which might make it sensible to have different levels of restriction?

TWO VIEWS OF PERMISSIVENESS

The Church, like many organizations at the time, was unsure whether to criticize the new trends in society or to follow them.

The Bishop of Blackburn, Dr. C.R. Claxton, has banned Bingo as a means of raising money for Church funds in his diocese.

Writers, artists and designers also broke away from traditional forms. Pop art came to Britain from America in the early 1960s. This was the realistic presentation of images drawn from such items of everyday life as comics and advertisements. An example of pop art is this portrait of Marilyn Monroe, "Marilyn" (1967), by the American Andy Warhol. © DACS 1985.

A month ago the Bishop of Manchester described Bingo as "A Boil on the Face of an Affluent Society". (*Sunday Times*, 16 July 1961)

Minister's wife Marjorie Janney, 29, wore a micro dress to Church yesterday. It was twelve inches above the knee. And she heard her husband in the pulpit hit at narrow-minded people who scorn "mod" gear.

Glamorous Mrs. Janney said – "they didn't like my mini-skirts." Then they were only six inches above the knee.

Mr. Janney was preaching at the eleventh anniversary of the Church he helped to build. "I have thrown my cassock away – often I don't even wear a clerical collar." And his wife joked – "I'm going to use his cassock for a maxi-skirt this winter." (*Daily Mail*, 9 September 1968)

Protest!

The Sixties was an angry and protesting generation. Protest took many different forms – both peaceful and violent demonstrations, songs and, in some cases, a complete rejection of society and its values. Targets for the protests were many and varied – from the capitalism of Western Europe and America to the Vietnam War.

BAN THE BOMB

The Campaign for Nuclear Disarmament (CND) attracted a large number of members in the late 1950s and staged an annual Easter march from the Aldermaston base (near Reading) to a rally in central London.

> **50,000 Ban the Bomb members shuffled into Trafalgar Square yesterday. Foot-sore, rain-soaked but undaunted, they were cheered in by another 5,000 waiting to greet them. Earlier the two columns of marchers from Aldermaston and Wethersfield NATO base in Essex converged to schedule. They streamed three by three, banners waving, up Whitehall behind a solo piper.**

> **The last speaker [in Trafalgar Square] was Mr Michael Foot MP. He forecast "a great victory against nuclear strategy at this year's Labour Party Conference in Blackpool".** (*Daily Mail*, 3 April 1961)

What do you know about the activities of CND in the 1980s?

THE VIETNAM WAR

All through the 1960s American troops fought in South East Asia to try to prevent the spread of Communism. Although the methods used by the Vietcong (Communist) guerillas could be very cruel, the heavy bombing of Communist cities in North Vietnam by the US Air Force was widely resented.

In 1945 Britain had 17 universities; by 1972 there were 44, many of them opened in the 1960s. The dramatic increase in student numbers was one reason for the increased volume of protest. Student protest slogans, Cambridge, early 1969.

▽

> **Daily one was shown on television the horrors of the war. Few people, I am sure, will ever forget the sight of the little girl running through the sea of flame; napalm had been dropped on her town, her clothes burnt off, her body scarred and burned. The Vietnamese people seemed to me to be so gentle. I felt personally their suffering and anger that the richest, most powerful nation in the world, the United States, could inflict such suffering on a poor and gentle people. I felt compelled to do something.**
>
> **Firstly, I collected for medical aid for Vietnam. Then, because I wanted to**

~~~~~~

AN ANTI-WAR PROTEST SONG

Come you masters of war, you that
    build all the guns
You that build the death planes, you
    that build the big bombs
You that hide behind walls, you that
    hide behind desks
I just want you to know I can see
    through your masks.

You that never done nothin' but build
    to destroy
You play with my world, like it's your
    little toy
You put a pen in my hand, and you hide
    from my eyes
And you turn and run farther when the
    fast bullets fly . . .
. . . You fasten the trigger for others to
    fire
Then you sit back and watch as the
    death count gets higher
You hide in your mansion as young
    people's blood
Flows out of their bodies and is buried
    in the mud.
(Bob Dylan)

Precisely whom do you think this song is criticizing?

At the end of the 1960s, the Hippy movement preached a gospel of Love, Peace and a return to Nature. This Punch *cartoon from 1972 pokes fun at the 1960s' hippy figures.*

I'M NOT SO SURE I SHOULD HAVE
GOT OUT
OF BED
THIS MORNIN'
THE CENTRAL HEATING OF MY
HEAD IS
TURNED OFF
AND LOOKING IN THE
MIRROR OF MY
MIND TO
SHAVE MY
GUILT AWAY
I WONDER ABOUT
THE AMERICAN
WAY OF
DEATH
THE LOON WITH
HIS FINGER ON
THE BUTTON
HOLDS THE KEY
TO LIFE
AND I'M LOCKED
OUT
I CROSS THE LEVEL
CROSSING OF MY
FINGERS
BUT THE LIGHTS ARE
AGAINST ME
THE BEST YEARS OF
OUR LIFE THEY SAY
BUT WERE THEY
CARRYING THE
WORLD ON THEIR
BACK
LIKE WE
DO?
LIKE HELL MAN!

I WROTE THIS BECAUSE THIS IS HOW I FEEL, YOU KNOW, ABOUT THE VILLAGE EARTH I CALL THE SONG — SONG ..... HERE GOES..... I HOPE YOU LIKE IT

make the war end, I joined in the huge demonstrations that were beginning to fill London's streets. More people than ever before were drawn to these demonstrations. I sold badges, gave out leaflets, sold papers, collected money and marched on demonstration after demonstration. Along with hundreds of others I picketed the US Embassy.

Never before had I felt such a complete sense of identification and involvement in anything I had done.

Did we do any good, the millions of us who protested over the war in Vietnam? There is no doubt that the massive protests in many countries helped to bring the war to an end. A US Senator, opposed to the war, was able to stand up in the Senate to announce that, "At this very moment our Embassy in London is under siege." I am very proud to have been a part of the protest which helped to end such an unjust war. (John Griffiths, born 1942)

Fashion

For some time after the Second World War most people had little money to spend on fashionable new clothes, and the materials to make them were very scarce. The new wealth of the late 1950s and early 1960s, combined with the desire everywhere to reject the ideas and designs of the past and to experiment boldly, led to some important fashion developments.

MEMORIES OF A TEENAGE GIRL

As a nearly-teenager in 1960, I was awkwardly weighed down with stockings and suspender-belts, vests and tummy-flattening girdles. The 1960s brought Freedom!

Hems began to rise . . . and rise. Our parents were horrified – where would it all stop? Schools tried to enforce the rule that skirts should be no more than two inches off the ground when kneeling down. But there seemed to be no end to the rise.

Tights took over from stockings, ending the embarrassing gap at the top of the legs which was always in danger of being revealed when we bent over. Leg-hugging plastic boots became our second skin.

Clothes were simple to wear and simple to make. The shift dress (only two pattern pieces) could be run up on a sewing machine in a couple of hours. Skinny-rib polo-neck jumpers and A-line mini-skirts were separated by belts of metal rings round waists which fell symmetrically halfway between neckline and hemline.

I longed to be the ideal shape for Sixties' clothes – a beanpole with matchstick legs – but I knew that I really had curves in the wrong places. In many ways the long skirts which became an alternative to mini-skirts in the late '60s were a welcome relief. (Joy James, born 1948)

MEMORIES OF A TEENAGE BOY

My main memory of early Sixties' fashion is the shoes. I had a great battle with my parents before I was allowed to buy the sort of suede shoes which would nowadays look very conventional indeed. Then the following year it was winkle-pickers (long, pointed shoes which were very uncomfortable). A year later the points had been chopped off an inch or two from the end and chisel-toes were all the rage – soon to be followed by Chelsea boots (with elastic sides) and Cuban (block) heels.

How I wish I had kept all my late Sixties clothes! But my blue Nehru-jacket (named after the Indian Prime Minister of the early '60s and of a type still worn in India today) looked very odd by the early '70s, and the vivid colours of the shirts and ties I bought in 1967 and 1968 no longer seemed very attractive. For a year or two every market had had a stall laden with ties made from the off-cuts of the multi-coloured dresses which were all the rage then. (Nigel Richardson, born 1948)

Why do you think parents and teachers were so opposed to all the fashion changes?

Men's fashion show, 1967.

CARNABY STREET

Carnaby Street in the West End of London became the headquarters of Sixties' fashion after John Stephen, a 19-year-old grocer's son came down from Glasgow to open his first clothes shop for teenagers.

In 1958 Mary Quant was one of the first to design clothes, shoes, make-up, hair styles for the under-20s, for whom London's Carnaby Street became a mecca.

New words like 'fab and gear' were used in shops (like 'Lord John's') where 'dolly' assistants wanted to serve the affluent young. The clothes were simple and, above all, they were relatively cheap. In the 1940s, Dior and others had catered for the very rich, and the less well-to-do had imitated these fashions. In the late 1950s designers catered for the 'classless' society of young people. The Dior revolutionary New Look had begun at the top of the income/age scale and then spread downwards: the Quant/Carnaby Street Revolution began with the young and spread upwards to older women, many of whom complained that they found it impossible to find a

A CHANGE IN TEACHERS' DRESS

At the beginning of the 1960s I can't imagine a teacher at my school wearing any shirt other than a white one. By the end of the 1960s there wasn't a white shirt to be seen anywhere. (Roy Collard, grammar school pupil, 1963-70)

shop to provide them with the clothes they needed – everyone seemed to be catering for the young. (From *A History of Post-War Britain* by Peter Lane, Macdonald Educational, 1971)

What do you think someone writing in this way in 2005, about the 1980s, will have to say about its fashions?

Punch, *4 December 1963. A sign of the times. As hairstyles got longer, more time had to be spent looking after them.*

"*I can't come out tonight, Doris— I'm washing my hair.*"

23

Television, Radio and Cinema

In 1955 4.5m television licences were issued. By 1965 the figure had reached 13.2m; by 1975 it was 17.7m. In the same 20-year period, admissions to cinemas went down from 1,935m to 124m. (After Bingo was made legal in 1960, many cinemas were turned into Bingo Halls.) The introduction of BBC2 in 1964 enabled television to cater more for minority tastes than in the past. Colour television was introduced in 1967, sending the cinemas into further decline. Radio was reorganized into four "home" channels in the late 1960s, catering for all tastes in Pop Music (Radio 1), Light Music and Entertainment (2), classical music (3) and current affairs and drama (4), while the World Service broadcast 700 hours of radio programmes each week in 40 languages.

THE FORSYTE SAGA

The BBC spent £300,000 making *The Forsyte Saga*, a 26-part serial based on novels by John Galsworthy. Set in an age long before TV was invented, it became a huge hit with BBC2 viewers and was eventually transferred to BBC1.

> **People organized their whole week around the next episode of 'The Forsyte Saga'; several of my friends never went out on the night on which it was shown, never invited anyone in, never even answered the phone while it was on. Part of the success of the series lay in**

DR WHO

On 21 November 1963, page 7 of the *Radio Times* previewed a new programme.

> **Dr. Who? That is just the point. Nobody knows precisely who he is, this mysterious exile from another world and a distant future whose adventures begin today. But this much is known: he has a ship which can travel through space and time – although, owing to a defect in its instruments, he can never be sure where and when his 'landings' may take place.**

Why do you think Dr Who has been so popular?

JULIA FOSTER —PLAY OF THE WEEK ITV, 9.10

BBC1

9.35-9.55 PURE MATHEMATICS.
10.00-10.20 MEN IN HISTORY: The Invaders. No. 2: Metals.
10.45-11.00 WATCH WITH MOTHER: Picture Book.
11.05-11.25 TELEVISION CLUB: Mum's New Job.
11.30-11.55 FOR SIXTH FORMS: Science Serves the Arts.
1.00 HEDDIW.
1.25 NEWS.
1.30-1.45 WATCH WITH MOTHER: Tales of the Riverbank.
2.05-2.25 GOING TO WORK: Laboratory Technician.
2.30-2.50 SIGNPOST: Workers in a Neighbourhood.
2.55-3.15 MIDDLE SCHOOL MATHEMATICS.
5.05 BLUE PETER.
5.30 RIPCORD.
5.55 NEWS.
6.05 TOWN AND AROUND; Weather (or Regional News).
6.30 SING ALONG.
7.00 TONIGHT.
7.35 IMAGE OF THE EAST: Travels in Thailand, Laos and Cambodia. No. 4: River Kwai.
8.00 BEWITCHED: 'Love Is Blind.'
8.25 PANORAMA.
9.15 NEWS.
9.25 PERRY MASON: 'The Case of the Careless Kidnapper.'
10.15 COME DANCING. Peter West introduces another round of the nationwide amateur dancing competition.
11.00 NEWS EXTRA; Weather.
11.10 LAWS OF DISORDER: Chemical change and thermodynamics.

BBC2

11.00-11.30 PLAY SCHOOL.
6.57 NEWS.
7.00 THE BEAT ROOM, with Paul Anka and Cliff Bennett.
7.30 PICK THE WINNER.
8.00 THE VIRGINIAN: 'Another's Footsteps.'
9.15 THE HUMAN SIDE: A Man's Worth—a look at what people think they should be paid in relation to what they are paid.
10.00 HIT AND RUN: Episode 2: 'Enquiry.'
10.30 NEWSROOM; Weather.
10.55 LATE NIGHT LINE-UP.

BBC WALES

AS LONDON, EXCEPT:
1.30 Ar Lin Mam. 6.05 Wales Today; Weather.
6.30 Heddiw. 6.55 Newyddion. 7.35 Stiwdio B.

LONDON ITV

11.30-11.48 THE WORLD AROUND US. No. 2: Metals.
2.05-2.25 FINDING OUT. Food—2.
2.28-2.53 ONE WORLD. My Country Right or Wrong.
4.20 SMALL TIME. Ivor the Engine and Muriel Young talks to Pussy Cat Willum.
4.35 CROSSROADS.
5.00 SEEING SPORT.
5.25 FLIPPER.
5.55 NEWS; Weather.
6.08 THAT'S FOR ME. Dan Farson and Anne Nightingale introduce June Christie, Val Doonican and Jessie Matthews.
7.00 ALL OUR YESTERDAYS.
7.30 CORONATION STREET.
8.00 CRANE. Patrick Allen, Sam Kydd, Gerald Flood and Laya Raki in 'The Man in the Gold Waistcoat.'
8.55 NEWS.
9.10 PLAY OF THE WEEK. 'The Image,' starring Julia Foster and Dinsdale Landen.
10.30 THE EXPLORERS. Jack Hargreaves talks to Ronald Lang.
11.00 NEWS HEADLINES.
11.02 DATELINE; Weather.
11.12 LIFE'S WORK. Celia Irving talks to Dr. H. A. Williams, Baptist.

REGIONAL ITV

AS LONDON, EXCEPT:

SOUTHERN: 5.25 Movie Magazine. 6.05 Day by Day. 6.45 Sports Desk. 11.02 News Extra. 11.10 Weather; Epilogue. 11.15 Post-Graduate Medicine.
MIDLANDS: 11.05 Wir Waren Vier. 4.45 Tingha and Tucker Club. 5.25 Mr. Piper. 6.05 News. 6.15 A TV Today. 6.35 Crossroads. 11.00 Ready, Steady, Go! 11.12 News. 11.16 Ready, Steady, Go! (cont.). 11.50 Dateline; Weather.
WALES and WEST: 2.25 One World. 4.00 Newyddion y Dydd. 4.05 Gwybod y Gair. 5.25 Movie Magazine. 6.05 T W W Reports. 6.13 Here Today. 6.30 Father of the Bride. 7.00 Discs a Gogo. 10.30 Mind Behind Crime. 11.15 Mr. Haydn meets Mr. Burns. 11.45 Weather.
WESTWARD: 4.38 News. 4.40 Gus Honeybun's Birthdays. 4.45 Small Time. 5.25 Mr. Ed. 6.05 Westward Diary. 6.20 Sports Desk. 6.35 Crossroads. 7.00 Discs a Gogo. 10.30 All Our Yesterdays. 11.02 News; Dateline. 11.15 Mr. Haydn meets Mr. Burns. 11.45 Weather; Faith for Life.
NORTHERN: 2.30 One World. 3.50 Towards 2000. 4.20 Management in Action. 5.25 Robin Hood. 6.05 Patty Duke. 6.30 Scene at 6.30. 11.02 Time Without Pity. 11.45 Granada in the North.
CHANNEL: 4.40 Puffin's Birthday Greetings. 4.45 Small Time. 5.25 Movie Magazine. 6.05 News; Weather. 6.15 Movie Museum. 6.30 Golf Tips No. 21. 6.35 Crossroads. 10.30 Citizens All. 11.01 News. 11.03 Post-Graduate Medicine. 11.53 Weather and News in French; Weather.
NORTH and WEST WALES: 2.25 One World. 5.25 Dringo'r Ysgol. 6.06 Y Dydd. 6.24 I'm Dickens, He's Fenster. 6.51 News. 7.00 Discs a Gogo. 10.30 Mind Behind Crime. 11.15 Mr. Haydn meets Mr. Burns. 11.45 Weather.

◁ *A typical Monday evening's viewing, 25 January 1965. Are any of these programmes still being broadcast today?*

the fact that the actors who played the children actually looked like the actors playing their parents. The long, peaceful scene in which the senior member of the family, Old Jolyon, drifts off to sleep and gently dies in a chair in his garden on a summer day is one of the most moving scenes I have ever seen on televsion. (Tim Ash, a teenager in 1967 when the serial was first shown)

FAMOUS 1960s' FILMS

1960 – *The Guns of Navarone*
       Psycho
1962 – *Lawrence of Arabia*
1963 – *The Birds*
       From Russia with Love
1964 – *Dr. Strangelove*
       A Hard Day's Night
1967 – *Bonnie and Clyde*
1968 – *2001: A Space Odyssey*
1969 – *Midnight Cowboy*
       Easy Rider

Many of these films were very exciting. Why did cinema audiences go down so much?

PIRATE RADIO

In the early 1960s, little pop music was broadcast by the BBC New broadcasting stations would have needed government permission, and the trade unions were not enthusiastic about too much broadcasting of pop records, in case record sales decreased. But in 1964 "Radio Caroline" began broadcasting as an unauthorised "pirate" station. Soon it was rivalling "Radio Luxemburg", with over 7m listeners. Other "pirate" stations followed, although most of them closed down after the Government refused to legalize them, and the BBC introduced Radio One in 1967.

Radio Caroline anchored off the Essex coast close to where I lived and worked. We weren't to know it at the time, but we were being involved in something revolutionary. For, from the moment Radio Caroline began to broadcast to us, the attitude towards pop music on the radio, as well as the very role of music in our lives, was going to change. We had never heard anything like it before: pop music non-stop round the clock and introduced in a familiar, jokey way by DJs influenced by American radio stations.

With the success of the "pirates", the BBC was forced to change its image. A whole channel was set aside to specialise in pop music with, to make public the defeat, many of the "pirate" DJs who had become "respectable".

Many well-known DJs learned their skills living in very cramped and difficult conditions on boats bobbing up and down in the North Sea. There was great rivalry between the different "pirates", which, on one occasion, erupted into fighting and almost real-life "piracy". But during storms, when the lives of the "pirates" were at risk, there was a great deal of mutual support.

Although I welcomed the arrival of the "pirates", and am transported back to that time whenever I hear Dionne Warwick's "Walk on By", I now feel the value of our lives has been diminished by the tyranny of constant music. (John Griffiths, born 1942)

The rise of Satire was one of the most distinctive features of Sixties' life. Satire – making individuals or organizations look ridiculous by poking fun at them – not only became very widespread, but also was aimed now at things previously regarded as too important to be ridiculed. The monarchy and the Church are two examples.

PRIVATE EYE

No. 141.
Friday
12 May 67   1/6

COMMON MARKET

THE GREAT DEBATE BEGINS

THAT WAS THE WEEK THAT WAS (TW3)

"TW3", as it was known, was launched by the BBC in November 1962 as a late-night TV satire show on Saturdays. Watched each week by an audience of over 12 million, its two series seemed to symbolize the revolt of the Younger Generation against the ideas and out-of-date values of the "Establishment" – the older generation who were then in positions of power. Many of TW3's cast had been at Oxford or Cambridge University; its anchor-man was the then unknown David Frost.

I was barely 14 years old when TW3 began, but my parents allowed me to stay up to watch it. I was too young to understand all the jokes in detail, but I remember a tremendous sense of excitement each week as the programme began – who would be the targets of the Satire this week? I don't remember my parents being shocked, but they were sometimes very surprised by just how daring the programme could be.

Two sketches have stayed in my mind. One was a commentary in which the Queen and her family travelled down the Thames in the Royal Barge which began to sink. Phrases from the "commentator" like "The Queen, smiling bravely, is now swimming for her life while Lord Snowdon takes a colour photograph" brought a gasp of amazement from the audience. The other very controversial item I remember was a "Consumer Guide to Religions". This was presented in the same way as *Which?* magazine compares different vacuum cleaners or fridges – what they do for you, whether they give good value for money and so on. Many viewers telephoned the BBC to complain.

Although I was only dimly aware of it at the time, I can honestly say that I did realize that this was something quite new in the history of Television. (Nigel Richardson, aged 14 in 1962)

Why do you think so many viewers complained?

For much of the 1960s a fierce political debate took place over whether Britain should join the Common Market (EEC). Private Eye commented satirically on the level of interest in this issue amongst ordinary people.

PRIVATE EYE

Private Eye was another 1960s' product, a fortnightly satire magazine which is still very popular today. One of its regular features in the 1960s was "Mrs Wilson's Diary" which was supposed to be written by the Prime Minister's wife. When the tanker *Torrey Canyon* sank near the Wilsons' holiday bungalow on the Isles of Scilly, *Private Eye's* diary contained the following "description" of Mr Wilson planning the operation to stop the oil-slick spreading:

Harold had transformed the lounge into a 'War Room' with a Readers' Digest Foldout Polar Map pinned to the wall with drawing pins. . . . Harold was standing by the map in his old Oxford duffle coat with Giles's Beatle-style George Lennon cap and old pair of gumboots he uses for gardening, and was moving little red flags about while the nautical gentlemen made gruff noises and remarked that it was just like old times. I was just opening another tin of Spam for a fork lunch when Jim Callaghan tapped on the kitchen window wearing a polo neck sweater and his old HMS Buffoon blazer on with a row of brightly polished medals pinned to his lapel. "Heave ho my hearties" he remarked, wiping his boots on the coconut matting, "Skipper on the bridge?" At this moment Harold appeared asking whether I could get down Robin's old Sink the Dreadnought Set from the attic, and move the folding card table into the lounge to represent the Atlantic Ocean. "Aha" cried Jim "I am ready to leave for Falmouth as soon as Audrey has got my bicycle up from the basement." "I don't think that will be necessary Jim," remarked Harold . . . "I myself, as you can see, am paramount commander of Operation Daz as we have dubbed it."

What are you meant to think about the Prime Minister by reading this passage?

Private Eye *did not have a very high opinion of politicians! How does this cartoon show that?*

"Good luck, Minister – and when you lie remember to look straight into the cameras!"

Some people might say that the Sixties was the "golden age" of Pop Music with such groups as The Shadows, The Dave Clark Five, Herman's Hermits, The Bachelors, Manfred Mann and The Who all recording well over a dozen hits, and such individual performers as Cliff Richard and Adam Faith remaining popular all through the decade. Cheap singles, and the fact that the records were played so often on radio and television, helped to make all these performers into household names. Two groups stand out – The Beatles and The Rolling Stones.

6.8 Ready, Steady, Go!

The Weekend Starts Here
KEITH FORDYCE
WITH
CATHY McGOWAN
invites you to meet a galaxy of guest stars, including
THE FOURMOST
THE ANIMALS
THE MOJOS
KING SIZE TAYLOR
THE PARAMOUNTS
SANDIE SHAW
PROGRAMME EDITOR
FRANCIS HITCHING
ASSISTANT VICKI WICKHAM
DIRECTED BY PAT LUMSDEN
Rediffusion Network Production

One of the most successful programmes about pop music was broadcast on ITV every Friday evening.

THE BEATLES

One of the 300 groups formed in Liverpool in 1960 was The Silver Beatles. They played regularly at the Cavern Club.... No fewer than five

TOP ARTISTS OF THE SIXTIES

1.	43 hits	Cliff Richard
2.	25	The Shadows
3.	24	Billy Fury
4.	23	Adam Faith, The Beatles
6.	20	The Hollies
7.	19	The Dave Clark Five
9.	17	Cilla Black, Herman's Hermits, The Bachelors, Sandie Shaw, Manfred Mann, Tom Jones
15.	16	Shirley Bassey, Dusty Springfield
17.	15	The Rolling Stones, Frank Ifield, The Kinks
20.	14	Kenny Ball, Ken Dodd, The Who

(From *Fab: The Sounds of the Sixties* by Tony Jasper, Blandford Press, 1984)

large recording companies turned down the chance of offering the Beatles a recording contract.... Their first single, 'Love Me Do' was released in October 1962.... From then on, events moved fast. (From *The Sixties* by Francis Wheen, Century Publishing with Channel 4 Television, 1982)

I shall never ever forget going to the Beatles Christmas show (at the Astoria Finsbury Park in 1962). We looked forward to it for days beforehand. On the night itself the atmosphere was electric as the other groups played in the first half of the concert. I particularly remember a young, then unknown singer from Liverpool called Cilla Black.

Suddenly there were John, Paul, George and Ringo dressed in grey

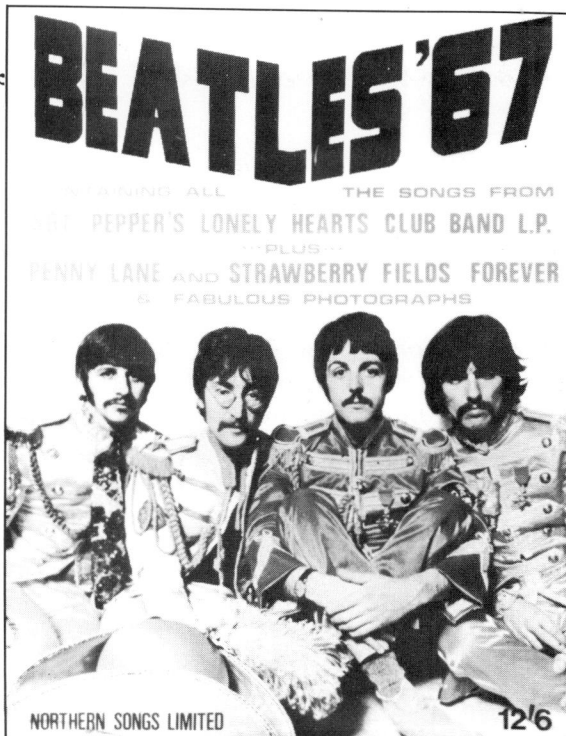

BEATLES '67

CONTAINING ALL THE SONGS FROM SGT. PEPPER'S LONELY HEARTS CLUB BAND L.P.

PLUS

PENNY LANE AND STRAWBERRY FIELDS FOREVER

& FABULOUS PHOTOGRAPHS

NORTHERN SONGS LIMITED   12/6

The Beatles in 1967.

THE BEATLES' SONGS

Read these two extracts from Beatles' songs – one from the early Sixties and one from the later years, and compare the photograph on this page with the picture of The Beatles on the front cover of this book. By the late 1960s The Beatles had come under the influence of the "flower power" drug culture and were studying Eastern mystical religions.

> **Close your eyes and I'll kiss you,**
> **tomorrow I'll miss you**
> **Remember we'll always be true**
> **And then while I'm away, I'll write**
> **home every day**
> **And I'll send all my loving to you.**
> ("All my loving")

> **When I get older, losing my hair, many**
> **years from now**
> **Will you still be sending me a Valentine,**
> **birthday greetings, bottle of wine?**
> **If I'd been out till quarter to three,**
> **would you lock the door?**
> **Will you still need me, will you still feed**
> **me when I'm 64?**
> ("When I'm sixty four")

What differences do you notice between the two songs?

> **Beatle jackets – Ringo's drums bearing**
> **the familiar lettering of The Beatles. All**
> **the girls started screaming. A few**
> **fainted; others tried to climb onto the**
> **seats or stood in the gangways doing**
> **the Twist. Afterwards, they had to turn**
> **fire-hoses on the crowd outside to stop**
> **them storming the stage door . . .**
> (Charles Gregory, born 1948)

Why do you think the Beatles were so popular?

THE ROLLING STONES

> **The limousine came up the street**
> **towards me and stopped directly**
> **outside the Odeon stage door. The**
> **police formed cordons. Then the car**
> **door opened and the Rolling Stones got**
> **out, all five of them and Andrew Loog**
> **Oldham, their manager, and they**
> **weren't real. They had hair down past**
> **their shoulders and they wore clothes**
> **of every colour imaginable and they**
> **looked mean, they looked just**
> **impossibly evil.**
>
> **In this grey street, they shone like sun**
> **gods. They didn't seem human, they**
> **were like creatures off another planet,**
> **impossible to reach or understand but**
> **most exotic, most beautiful in their**
> **ugliness.**
> (From *AwopBopalooBoplopBamBoom* by
> Nik Cohn, Paladin, 1970)

Thanks to Television, millions of people saw the great sporting moments of the 1960s — far more than had seen similar events in earlier decades. With the increasing use of communications satellites to "bounce" TV pictures from one continent to another, sports events were often seen live. Earlier audiences had had to wait hours, or even days, after an event was over and after radio or TV news had told them the result, before they actually saw how the result was achieved.

FOOTBALL – WINNING THE WORLD CUP

My last school Speech Day took place on the afternoon of the World Cup quarter-finals. Immediately after the Headmaster's speech, I was amazed when the half-time scores were announced. I'm sure it would not have been done ten years earlier, and I remember thinking that this was a sign of how things were changing. England were still 0–0 against Argentina, but a huge cheer went up for the real outsiders, North Korea, who were leading Italy 3–2. (They lost 3–5).

A week later, I was on holiday in Cornwall. Like many others I stood in Wadebridge High Street and watched the final on a set in the window of a TV rental shop. Huge traffic queues built up as drivers stopped to ask us the score. (Nigel Richardson, aged 18 in 1966)

Can your father or mother tell you where *they* saw the Final?

Martin Peters scores England's second goal in the ▷ *World Cup final, 1966. Geoff Hurst (number 21) runs in to congratulate him.*

TENNIS

In 1968, Wimbledon allowed professional tennis players to take part for the first time. British tennis players did not generally do well there in the 1960s, although Angela Mortimer won the ladies' singles title in 1961.

Ann Jones triumphed at last yesterday to win the Wimbledon Singles title that eluded her so long. Then she said of her

BRAVE ENGLAND DO IT BUT OH! THE HEARTACHE

By Brian Glanville, Wembley.
England 4 (1)   West Germany 2 (1)
Scorers: Hurst (3), Peters, for England
           Haller, Weber, for Germany
After extra time – 90 minutes 2–2.
England, after the heartache and a thousand natural shocks of an astonishing game, have won the World Cup. . . . In effect, they won the final twice; won it, quite on their merit, in ordinary time, won it again in extra time, after a flagrantly illegal German goal had been allowed in the last minute . . . (*Sunday Times*, 31 July 1966)

defeat of Billie Jean King in her second Wimbledon final: "I was in a dream all the time".

Victory came to 30 year old Mrs. Jones after years of trying by 3–6, 6–3, 6–2. It brought her a standing ovation from the packed Centre Court, headed by a five-strong Royal Party. (*Daily Mail*, 5 July 1969)

BOXING

Cassius Clay (later known as Muhammed Ali) was a black American heavyweight who became champion of the world. He was known as the "Louisville Lip" after the city he came from and because of his boast, "I am the greatest".

COOPER FALLS IN FIVE!
CUT EYE JINX CATCHES UP WITH BRAVE HENRY

By Tom Phillips

Cassius Clay stopped Henry Cooper in five rounds at Wembley Stadium last night – just as he promised. But the British and Empire Heavyweight champion was so near to ramming the Louisville Lip's pre-fight words down his throat.

Clay won when referee Tommy Little stepped in to lead a half-blind Cooper back to his corner with blood streaming from a jagged gash over his left eye. The cut jinx had beaten Cooper again! Yet it might have been such a different story but for the bell at the end of the fourth round.

Clay was on the canvas. Cooper had

TEN PIN BOWLING

A classic, short-lived sporting craze of the 1960s was ten-pin bowling. The first Bowl opened in Britain in 1960.

We often went ten-pin bowling on Saturday evenings in the 1960s. There were at least six alleys within 25 miles of my home in North London. Four of us would go over and we would perhaps play three full games in an hour and a quarter. There was a huge variety of people there – some who looked as if they went every night. They had their own balls, shoes and special clothes and scored strikes (all ten-pins down at the first attempt) every time. Others were complete beginners – occasionally you would see someone who couldn't even manage to roll the ball as far as the pins, or whose ball crashed into the machinery if they bowled it when the gate was down. (John Hartley, born 1941)

Where have all the ten-pin bowlers gone? That's the question senior executives of Rank's are asking. Despite bold prophecies that this American family game would catch on in this country, the organisation's ten-pin bowling division is going out of business ... (*Leicester Mercury*, 3 October 1969)

Why do you think this craze lasted such a short time?

dropped him with a left hook – bang on the chin. The count reached three. Then the bell clanged to reprieve Cassius. (*Daily Herald*, 19 June 1963)

Rail and Road

In the 1960s the number of licensed road vehicles grew from 9.4m to 14.8m. These ten years also saw a rapid growth in motorway-building and main-road improvements. At the same time, the number of people wanting to travel by rail, or to send goods by train, dropped sharply. As the railways lost money, 1,850 stations closed between 1958 and 1963, the year in which Dr Beeching produced his plan to close 5,000 miles of track — about one third of the total rail mileage in Britain — and another 2,100 stations. Some railways were actually turned into roads.

PASSENGERS NO MORE

Michael Flanders and Donald Swann wrote a famous song called "The Slow Train", which listed some of the unusual-sounding names of stations where trains would no longer call:

> . . . On the main line and the goods
> siding the grass grows high
> At Dogdyke, Tumby Woodside and
> Troublehouse Halt.
> The sleepers sleep at Audlem and
> Ambergate.
> No passenger waits on Chidling
> Platform for Cheslyn Hay.
> No-one departs; no-one arrives – From
> Selby to Goole
> From St Erth to St Ives.
> They've all passed out of our lives
> On the Slow Train . . .

Why does this song sound so sad?

A BRANCH LINE CLOSES

The branch line from Whitland to Cardigan in South West Wales closed on Saturday, 8 September 1962.

> The one-coach trains were quaint but unprofitable survivors of a bygone age. In the final months passengers dropped to a handful as households in the Taff Vale . . . turned to private transport. . . . On the final day people all along the line turned out in force to see the end of their railway. The 5.45 pm with four coaches . . . had to stop twice at many of the stations where the platforms were not long enough. The following day . . . all the signals were taken out of use . . .

A typical branch line station casualty of the 1960s – Hallaton, Leicestershire. Both the passengers and the track have long since gone.

THE M1 OPENS

The M1, Britain's first motorway, opened in 1959. By 1970, much of central Britain was served by motorways, and the construction of several vital bridges (for example, over the Severn near Bristol and over the Forth near Edinburgh) greatly shortened journey times. The high level of accidents in the early years led to the introduction of a 70mph speed limit.

Mr. Ernest Marples, Minister of Transport, opened the £22m 72-mile London–Birmingham motorway today. And then, at a celebration lunch in London, he gave his verdict on the first drivers to use it. He said "I was really

APPALLED at the speed some of those cars were travelling . . . drivers must not forget that it is not a matter of skill alone on the motorway . . . there must be discipline and judgement. . . . If necessary we shall have to consider such things as a maximum speed limit . . .

3000 vehicles used the motorway in the first two hours. Average car speed was anything from 60-90 mph. (*London Evening Standard*, 3 November 1959)

lifting of the track was complete the following summer. (From *The Railways of Pembrokeshire* by John Morris, H.G. Walters (Publishers) Ltd, Tenby, 1981)

Can you discover the routes of any railways in your area which closed in the 1960s?

Country areas lost most of their railways. In the southwest, all these lines were open in 1960. By mid-1970 all the dotted ones had closed.

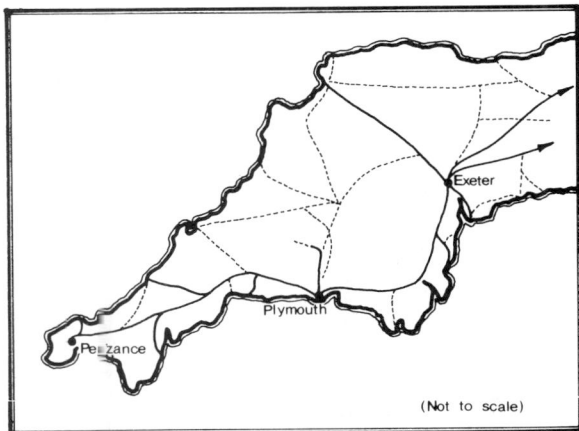

(Not to scale)

A FIRST MOTORWAY JOURNEY

I first went on a motorway in 1965 (as a passenger in a friend's car). We lived in Kent and were going on holiday in Northumberland, so the M1 made a lot of difference to us. We got to Yorkshire in time for lunch, which seemed marvellous then.

In those days, there was less traffic and motorway driving was more restful. There were no roadworks either! We had a smooth, fast ride. I remember admiring the bridges over the road, which looked very modern and elegant. I also remember the service-station where we stopped for a coffee. I had never seen one before, though my friend had, in the U.S.A. They were still very clean and shining in 1965, and I was much impressed; you could park easily, get something to eat, shop and be on your way quickly again. I especially noticed the hot-air machines for drying your hands in the Ladies – I'd never seen those before either. (Dr Madeline Jones)

Law and Order

During the 1960s crime increased steadily, especially in cities. There was a particular increase in crimes of violence. The abolition of hanging in 1965 was hotly argued inside and outside Parliament. Up till then, criminals could be hanged for certain types of murder — for example, shooting a policeman during a robbery. The newspapers claimed that the Great Train Robbery of 1963, the single most dramatic crime of the 1960s, was an example of a crime carried out by a new breed of professional, expert criminal.

KNOWN OFFENCES IN ENGLAND AND WALES

1955 − 438,085	1970 − 1,555,994
1960 − 806,900	1975 − 2,105,631
1965 − 1,331,882	(HMSO report)

Why is it important to say these are figures for "known" offences?

THE EXECUTION OF A CONVICTED MURDERER

All was quiet inside and outside Bedford Jail today as James Hanratty was hanged for murder. About 200 people stood in silence outside the jail gates as Hanratty went to the gallows at 8.00 am. The extra police on duty were not needed. A few minutes after the execution, a uniformed police inspector came out of the jail and said quietly "It is all over". . . . As the crowd began to drift away, a man stepped forward and placed a bunch of flowers by the prison doors . . . (*Evening Standard*, 4 April 1962)

Why do you think the crowd had gathered outside the jail?

MURDER ON A SUMMER AFTERNOON

3 police officers were shot dead in Braybrook Street, Shepherds Bush (West London) this afternoon. . . . The shooting happened after a car containing four men had been followed by the police. . . . I saw one body lying ten yards from the police car. Another was slumped in the seat of the car. A third was underneath. The windscreen of the car was shattered. A hundred policemen rushed to the scene and cordoned off the area.

Mr Duncan Sandys, Tory MP for Streatham, declared . . . "As soon as Parliament reassembles, I intend to demand the restoration of hanging for the killing of policemen and jailers. . ."
(*Evening Standard*, 13 August 1966)

Why do you think Mr Sandys wanted to restore hanging? Do you agree with him?

SOME TYPICAL PRISON CELL RULES

- Cells are to be left clean and tidy at all times.
- Beds are to be made by 0700.
- Water will be drawn at 0700 and 1300 only.
- When entering the Wing from exercise or labour, go straight to your cell and close the door. DO NOT WANDER ABOUT THE LANDING changing books and talking.
- "Pin ups" are not to be stuck on the wall; use the board that is provided.

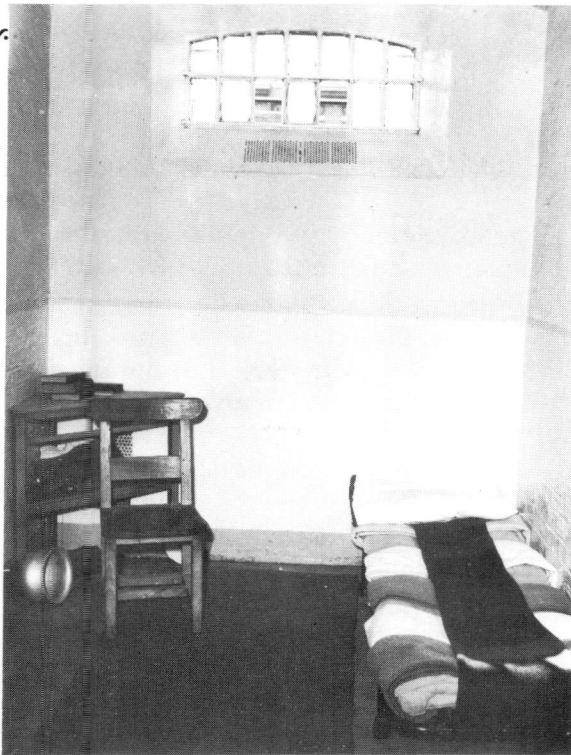

A typical cell at Wormwood Scrubs, 1966.

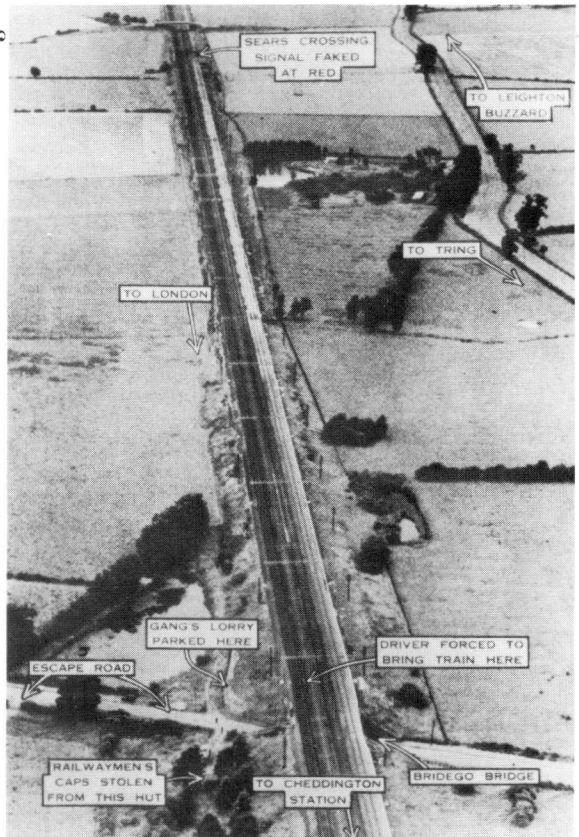

This Daily Telegraph *photograph shows in detail how the Great Train Robbery was carried out. It was highly planned and carried out with great precision. Most of the missing money has never been recovered.*

1963: £1m STOLEN IN GREAT TRAIN ROBBERY

A worn brown glove and four large torch batteries were all the equipment used by a gang who ambushed a GPO mail train near here early today and carried out the biggest and most audacious train robbery in British history.

Late last night Det. Supt. Fewtrell, head of Bucks C.I.D., described the amount taken as "clearly well over £1m".

The gang, armed and masked with balaclavas and scarves and believed to number between eight and fifteen, operated with split-second timing. They:

– Tampered with a long-distance signal;
– Set another automatic signal on the main line between Leighton Buzzard and Cheddington stations at red;
– Stopped the train, known as the Travelling Post Office, split it in two and coshed the driver, handcuffing him to the co-driver;
– Escaped with about 120 mailbags containing over £1 million. (Guy Rais, *Daily Telegraph*, 9 August 1963)

Some of the gang were later sentenced to 30 years in prison, although none of them actually served that long. The engine driver was permanently disabled and died in 1970. What do you think would have been a suitable sentence for the robbers?

Race Relations

By 1966 the number of black Britons was 924,000. Most of these people had come to Britain from the West Indies, India and Pakistan, although during the 1960s a significant number of immigrants came from Kenya and Uganda. The African governments of these countries drove out citizens of Asian origin, who played a leading role in the economies of Kenya and Uganda, accusing them of depriving Africans of jobs.

Many of the newcomers to Britain made their homes in cities where the demand for labour was high, especially London, Birmingham, Leicester, Bradford and Wolverhampton. A large number found employment in hospitals or on the buses, jobs which the white population was unwilling to take up. Many whites accused the immigrants of accepting work for very low rates of pay, thus forcing whites to do the same. The newcomers were also blamed for long housing waiting lists. On the other hand, many white Britons disagreed with the politician, Enoch Powell's gloomy predictions of violence to come.

British governments passed Immigration Acts in 1962 and 1968, restricting further entries. Faced with increasing evidence that those already here were suffering discrimination in jobs and housing, Parliament also passed Race Relations Acts in 1965 and 1968, to help ensure equal treatment for all citizens.

NEW ARRIVALS

Many Asian families had to flee from Kenya in 1968.

Hashid does not look like a refugee, but had his father not acted quickly, he might be one by now. Mr. J. T. Patel saw the trouble [in Kenya] coming last July,

PARLIAMENT RESTRICTS IMMIGRATION

The Commonwealth Immigrants Act was read the third time in the House of Lords at 8.50 yesterday morning and passed eight minutes later. An hour later the Lord Chancellor announced that the Bill had been given the Royal Assent.

The peers had debated throughout the night the controversial measure that will cut the flow from Kenya of Asian immigrants to Britain.

Lord Shepherd for the government denied that the Bill was a racialist measure. There is a limit to the numbers we can absorb and there is a greater limit as to the rate at which we can absorb immigrants of any class or colour. We are dedicated to a multi-racial society.

so he took a working holiday to England and bought a grocer's shop in Charlotte Place, W1. "Things were getting very hard for us in Kenya, trading was affected, the children's education was threatened, so I came over here, paid the deposit on this business, and went back to Nairobi to collect my family."

The shelves of his shop are stocked to overflowing. Both Mr. and Mrs. Patel are on first name terms with their customers. "My two children are at school up by the Post Office Tower. They are very happy there and have many friends. I am happy to say that most people in England treat us all as equals." (*Illustrated London News,* 20 April 1968)

The man in the dock is Home Secretary, James ▷
Callaghan, the minister responsible for immigration.
The new Race Relations law and the act limiting
Commonwealth immigration came at much the same
time. What point is the cartoon trying to make?

Baroness Wootton said the price we
should have to pay for this Bill was a
sacrifice that would bring shame to the
supporters of this government and
which would do irreparable damage to
the moral image of the senior partner in
the British Commonwealth. (*The
Guardian*, 2 March 1968)

THE NEW RACE RELATIONS LAW — Case No. 1

"It shall be unlawful for any person . . . . to practise discrimination on the ground of colour, race, ethnic or national origins."

HOW ARE ASIANS DOING OVER HERE?

Mr. Nathaniel Mahi arrived here from
Uganda on the Tuesday before the
Immigration Act came into effect. He
had worked in the Government
Education Service in Kenya and had
been headmaster of a private school
there.

Mr. Mahi's hardest task is to find
himself a job. He has 20 years'
experience as a teacher and
headmaster taking students up to 0
level. He has a BA degree awarded by
the authorities of the British Raj in
1947, and the British Government
accepted that degree as a teaching
qualification when they recruited him
from India for the Uganda Education
Service. In 1951-2 he spent a year at
London University and was awarded a
Diploma of Education to teach English.
But now he has been told he is not
recognised as qualified to teach here.

"In my first week I went to the
Labour Exchange and told them about
my degree, diploma, and experience. I
told them in Uganda I taught and was in
charge of teachers, observing and
giving guidance. They got in touch with
the Education Officer at Uxbridge who
said I must get a letter of recognition
from the Department of Education and
Science at Stanmore. I went to
Stanmore and they said 'Sorry. We
can't register you.' I said 'Look. You
registered me to teach in your service in
Uganda. You have recognised students
taught by me and accepted them for
higher education in this country, and
the newspapers here say there is a
shortage of teachers.' They said 'Sorry.
New regulations'".

The new regulations state that the
Department of Education and Science
no longer recognises ordinary degrees
from India and Pakistan as
qualifications sufficient for teaching in
this country. (Robert Lacey, *Illustrated
London News,* 20 April 1968)

The Disunited Kingdom?

Towards the end of the 1960s there was a growing feeling in Scotland and Wales that neither Conservative nor Labour politicians knew or cared much about problems in areas far from London. There was also a feeling that Scotland and Wales were missing out on the new prosperity enjoyed in South-East England. The population of country areas was decreasing, as young people moved away to towns in South-East England in search of jobs. The Scottish and Welsh Nationalist Parties wanted independence from England Plaid Cymru, the Welsh Nationalist Party, won a sensational by-election victory in Carmarthen in July 1966. Meanwhile, there was an increasingly tense situation in Northern Ireland.

SCOTLAND DEALS A BITTER BLOW TO MR WILSON

In 1967, the Scottish Nationalists won their first parliamentary seat for 22 years, in the Hamilton area of Glasgow.

The rising tide of Scottish Nationalism sensationally swept Labour out of Hamilton last night. A Labour majority of 16,756 at the General Election was transformed by Mrs. Winifred Ewing into a 1799 Scottish Nationalist triumph. The Tories lost their deposit in the Scottish seat. The message is plain for all Scottish MPs. Mrs. Ewing becomes the only Scottish Nationalist MP at Westminster but all three of the other parties have been told that they ignore Scottish Nationalist aspirations at their peril.

Mrs. Winifred Ewing (SNP)	18,397
A. Wilson (Labour)	16,598
I. Dyer (Conservative)	4,896

A jubilant Mrs. Ewing, a 38-year old Glasgow solicitor, said "Hamilton has made history for Scotland tonight. We will have a full-time home based Government by 1970". She left the hall to a fantastic reception from hundreds of young supporters who had waited more than 3 hours in teeming rain. She was greeted with chants of "Easy, easy". (*The Scotsman*, 3 November 1967)

Can you discover how well the Nationalist Parties have done in elections since 1967? Was Mrs Ewing correct to say that this result "made history"?

THE ROYAL INVESTITURE

In July 1969, the Investiture of Prince Charles as Prince of Wales took place in Caernarvon Castle. The ceremony was conducted by the Queen.

A bomb was found last night on the A5 trunk road near Holyhead, 45 minutes before the Prince of Wales's motorcade was due. (*Daily Mail*, 2 July 1969)
For two hundred miles and ten hours yesterday the Prince of Wales was greeted with cheers and waves. The ordinary people of Wales took him to their friendly hearts as he toured towns and villages from Llandudno to Fishguard. (*Daily Mail*, 3 July 1969)

Can you explain why protestors planted the bomb?

NORTH TO ELIZABETHA

The Economist magazine put forward one solution to the problems of declining areas:

> **What has the South of Britain got that the North really wants? Short answer: the economic and social stimulus of a London. What has the South got that it would be well rid of? Short answer: the inefficiency of a congested central London.**
>
> **We therefore propose as follows: to start building a new administrative capital for Britain – somewhere North of the Trent, and to move Queen, Parliament and civil service into it. A site on, say, the open building land between York and Harrogate might best fit the bill.**
>
> **The new city of Elizabetha would be the greatest single enterprise in Britain in modern architecture and town planning. It would give the North much closer contact with, and influence on,** **government. It would give London the opportunity to become again an efficient port poised to make the most of a Channel bridge or tunnel or dam with the continent.** (*The Economist,* 8 December 1962)

Do the problems mentioned in this article still apply to parts of Britain today?

Ireland was divided into two parts in the 1920s. Forty ▷ years later Southern Ireland, with a population which was almost entirely Roman Catholic, was an independent country. Northern Ireland (Ulster), with a Protestant majority, was still part of the United Kingdom.

Violence exploded in Ulster in the late 1960s and British troops were sent there. The Roman Catholics, who made up one-third of the population, protested that they were not given equal opportunities in jobs and housing. The Protestants accused them of helping the IRA, a terrorist organization determined to achieve a united Ireland by driving out the British.

The picture shows violence in Londonderry, August 1969. Police shelter behind the door of an armoured vehicle during a battle between stone-throwing mobs in the Roman Catholic Bogside area.

New Ideas

There has been plenty of evidence in the pages of this book to show that the 1960s was a time of new ideas, when many traditions and existing ways of doing things were put under close examination. Not all the changes of the 1960s a) look now as if they were for the better, b) lasted very long or c) came to anything in the end. Can you find any examples of these three things in the stories below?

A new design of car which transformed motoring ▷ habits: the transverse-engined mini. (An advertisement from 1964).

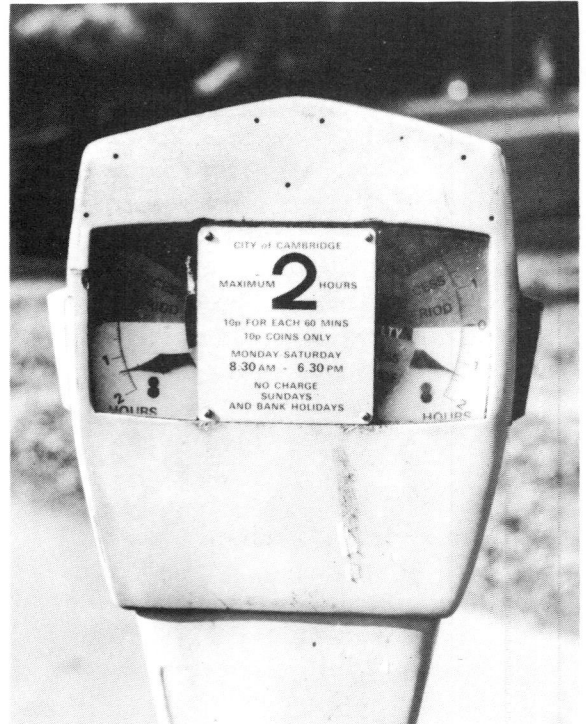

Another new arrival of the 1960s – the Parking Meter.

DECIMAL COINAGE

Britons will still be able to count their pounds and pence after D for Decimal Day in 1971. But the familiar 3d, 6d, 2/6d pieces will vanish for ever.

A government White Paper yesterday gave the expected go ahead for the pound-pence system, with 100 new pennies to the pound. (*The Sun*, 13 December 1966)

BRITISH SUMMER TIME – ALL THE YEAR ROUND

Clocks and watches go back an hour at 2.00 am tomorrow for the last time. They will go forward again on February 18th and from then on Britain will live by summer time all the year round. (*Daily Mail*, 28 October 1967)

Why do you think the change was timed to take place at 2 am?

A TWO-TIER POSTAL SYSTEM

A two-tier system for inland letters would be introduced on September 16th whereby "customers would pay according to the speed of the service they want...". The full-paid letter rate would be replaced by first and second class letter rates (minima 5d and 4d respectively up to 4 oz). Mr. Mason explained that second class letters might be subject to delays of up to 24 hours as compared with first class mail ... (*Keesings Contemporary Archives*, April 1968)

Why do you think a two-tier system would have helped the Post Office?

A CHANNEL TUNNEL?

The final report of the Channel Tunnel Study Group recommending the linking of Britain and France by a system of railway tracks at a cost of £109m was published on April 20th. (*Keesings Contemporary Archives*, April 1960)

WOMEN'S LIBERATION

(Man and Woman talking).
- What's the matter?
- It's my wife. She says she's going out to work.
- Well? That's nice for her.
- It's not nice for me. I don't want to come home to a dirty house and a dinner out of an old tin can, do I? And what about the children? Poor little latchkey mites . . .
- Both hefty teenagers!
- Running a home is a full-time job.
- It's not, you know. . . .
- Well it ought to be. . . .

(From "Loophole" ITC 1968, shown on Channel 4: *The Sixties*, Part 6)

NEW SIXTIES' WORDS AND PHRASES

See how many of the following you recognize, and ask people the meanings of the ones you don't. See if they can suggest others to add to the list.

ADJUSTING TO CHANGE

Sydney Carter, a notable religious song- and hymn-writer of the 1960s (you may know his "Lord of the Dance"), wrote an amusing song about how the Church tried to adapt in a time of change:

> "Good morning", said the Vicar,
> With a banjo round his neck,
> "We're digging up the crypt," he said,
> "To make a discotheque."
>
> So we're writing to the bishop
> To say that we are shocked.
> The vicar is a beatnik
> And he ought to be de-frocked.
>
> At early morning service
> He plays a mandoline.
> I'm never there to hear it,
> But I think it is a sin.
>
> So we're writing to the bishop
> To say that we are shocked.
> The vicar is a beatnik
> And he ought to be de-frocked.

(From *Songs of Sydney Carter, Book 1*, Stainer and Bell Ltd)

What attitude do you think this song is meant to make you have about the people who complained?

Some of them are mentioned in this book; some are old words with special meanings.

Boutique	Gear	Stop-Go
Cool	Groovy	Swinging
Demo	Grotty	Teach-In
Denim	Kinky	Topless
Disco	Op-Art	Trendy
Escalation	Pseud	Unisex
Fab	Psychedelic	Wage Freeze
Flower Power	Skinhead	With-It

The World in Your Living Room

One of the most important new things about life in the Sixties was that people could see dramatic pictures of events almost as soon as they happened, or even as they actually took place. Previously, people had relied on newspapers to tell them major news — in printed form, often a day or two after the event. The introduction of more portable television equipment and the invention of communications satellites like Telstar (1962) meant that people could watch horrifying wars, erupting volcanoes, or great sporting events and almost feel that they were at the scene themselves. Pictures of the violence in Northern Ireland and in Vietnam caused special shock amongst British viewers.

ABERFAN: DISASTER HITS A WELSH SCHOOL

About 150 people, including a "whole generation" of school children are missing or dead after the landslip disaster here today. It happened when an avalanche of pit waste slid down a mountain side and engulfed a school and houses in this mining village six miles from Merthyr Tydfil. . . . It was 9.15 and the school had just finished morning prayers when the million tons of coal, waste, rocks and water crumpled 800 feet down the Aberfan mountain. The children were due to start their week's half-term holiday at noon. (Denis Frost, *The Guardian*, 22 October 1966)

Aberfan had a tremendous impact on us at school, far away in South-East

THE RUSSIANS INVADE CZECHOSLOVAKIA

In 1968 Russian tanks entered Prague, Czechoslovakia to install a government more favourable to Moscow's ideas. Many Czech students were abroad at the time. Peter de Voil was working in a language school in Cambridge when news of the Russian invasion came through.

The news came first with a telephone call to one of the students from Prague. There was a stunned disbelief, shock and silence. Czech students talked quietly in groups, waiting for TV news broadcasts with tears running down their cheeks. All we could offer was sympathy; no-one knew the purpose and extent of the invasion, although when many of us remembered what had happened in Hungary in 1956 we were very fearful. I don't think any of them thought about staying in the West (they were 17-19 years old), but a few wondered if they would be allowed back into Czechoslovakia to rejoin their families. (Peter de Voil, born 1944)

Can you find out what happened in Hungary in 1956?

England. We immediately began a collection for the grief-stricken parents whom we had seen on TV. Normally, a school collection raised £5-10; within two days we had over £60, with more coming in all the time. (Nigel Richardson, 18 years old in 1966)

THE CUBAN MISSILE CRISIS

For a few days in October 1962 there seemed every chance that a nuclear war between the USA and the Soviet Union would begin in which all humankind would perish.

President John Kennedy announced to the world the discovery of missiles in Cuba, put there by the Soviet Union, capable of reaching targets well into the United States. Kennedy called on the Soviet Chairman, Nikita Kruschev, to end what he saw as a threat to peace by removing the missiles. Kennedy's message was broadcast on British radio.

Listening to it, late at night, with my family, I found myself faced with difficulties I had not experienced before. My parents were sure that Kennedy was "right", Kruschev "wrong" in putting missiles in Cuba. Like many people, I was fearful of the use of nuclear weapons and their spread around the world. At the same time, I had taken an interest in Cuba and was aware that the US government had organized an invasion of that country just a year before. Cuba, I felt, had a right to defend itself.

Kruschev finally agreed to take the missiles out of Cuba. We didn't know it at the time, but Kennedy had agreed, in return, never to invade Cuba. (John Griffiths, born 1942)

PRESIDENT KENNEDY DIES

President John F. Kennedy was shot dead in Dallas, Texas in November 1963.

There is hardly anyone alive who can't tell you what they were doing when they heard the news. I was sitting at the kitchen table with my father, struggling as usual with my maths homework. Suddenly my mother came into the room. I had hardly ever seen her crying before. There had just been a newsflash to say that the President was very seriously hurt. A few minutes later we were told that he was dead. He was so young, and he had somehow symbolized all the youthful optimism of the 1960s. (Peter Vincent, born 1948)

Ask people you know where *they* were that evening.

My form master in 1962-3 was a very fierce man who taught me Latin. It was always very difficult to get him off the subject (unlike some of the other masters who taught me) and, as we knew he was a very sick man, we did not try to do so very often.

I can only remember one occasion when he agreed to take up the red herring we offered him – on one day during the Cuban Missile crisis. We spent the whole lesson discussing whether there really would be nuclear war or not. Then I remember that we all sat around in our classroom at break just wondering whether we would all be here tomorrow. I have never felt quite like that, either before or since. . . . (Nigel Richardson, aged 14 in 1962)

Lossiemouth

NORTH SEA

Clydebank
Glasgow
Edinburgh

Londonderry

Belfast

IRISH SEA

Harrogate • • York
Blackpool • Blackburn
• Manchester
Holyhead • Liverpool
Llandudno
Caernarvon • Crewe

Nottingham •

Leicester •

Birmingham • Wethersfield
Thaxted
Bedford • Cambridge

Cardigan
Fishguard
Carmarthen Leighton Buzzard • Stansted
Whitland Merthyr Tydfil Wembley • Stanmore
Aberfan Uxbridge
Aldermaston ● LONDON
Bristol Streatham
Wimbledon

Hastings
Brighton

Wadebridge Bournemouth

ENGLISH CHANNEL

Land's End
Isles of
Scilly

0   100
Km

1960 Labour Party split over nuclear weapons.
Heart pacemaker developed by surgeons in Birmingham.
Split between China and Russia.
American U2 spy plane shot down over Russia.
Bloody Civil War in the Congo (in Africa) after it became independent from Belgium.
Massacre of 67 Africans at Sharpeville, South Africa, during a demonstration.

1961 The Portland Spy Case: Gordon Lonsdale, George Blake and Peter and Helen Kroger receive long prison sentences for spying for Russia.
John F. Kennedy becomes President of the USA.
South Africa leaves the Commonwealth because of her policy of apartheid (separate development for different races).
East Germans build the Berlin Wall to prevent people fleeing to the West.

1962 Death of Marilyn Monroe.

1963 Very severe winter in Britain.
Sir Alec Douglas Home succeeds Harold Macmillan as Prime Minister (Conservative).
France rejects Britain's application to join the EEC.
First woman (a Russian, Valentina Tereshkova) in space.

1964 Labour Party wins General Election: Harold Wilson becomes Prime Minister. Kruschev forced out of office in Russia; new government led by Brezhnev and Kosygin.

1965 Death of Sir Winston Churchill.
Edward Heath becomes Conservative Party leader.
Rhodesia's White Government led by Ian Smith declares itself illegally independent of Great Britain, rather than accept black majority rule.

1966 Harold Wilson and Labour Party win General Election.
Mrs Gandhi becomes Indian Prime Minister.

1967 Jeremy Thorpe succeeds Jo Grimond as Liberal Party leader.
Christian crusade by Billy Graham at Earls Court, London.
Right-wing army coup in Greece.
Six Day War between Israel and Egypt.
Communist guerilla leader Ché Guevara killed in Bolivia.

1968 Martin Luther King and Robert Kennedy assassinated in the USA.
Major student riots in Britain, America and many European countries.

1969 Richard Nixon succeeds Lyndon Johnson as American President.
French President de Gaulle resigns.

Biographical Notes

BARNARD Christiaan Neethling (born 1922). Professor of Surgical Science at Cape Town University 1968-83, he performed the world's first human heart transplant in December 1967 in Cape Town. The patient, Louis Washkansky, died after eighteen days, but the operation enjoyed an increasing success rate in subsequent years. Prof. Barnard also performed the world's first double-heart transplant in 1974. His books include *One Life* (1969) and *Heart Attack: You don't have to Die* (1971).

BEATLES John Lennon (1940-80), Ringo Starr (Richard Starkey born 1940), Paul McCartney (born 1942) and George Harrison (born 1943). One of the most successful British pop groups of all time, they came from Liverpool, where many of their early performances were given at the Cavern Club. They had eleven number one hits in a row, and seventeen in all, including "She Loves You" (1963), "Can't Buy Me Love" (1964) and "Yellow Submarine"/ "Eleanor Rigby" (1966). They developed rock music in notable new directions in *Sergeant Pepper's Lonely Hearts Club Band* (1967) but disbanded in 1970.

CHURCHILL Sir Winston Leonard Spencer (1874-1965). Journalist and politician, he first came to prominence as a reporter in the Boer War, before being elected to Parliament in 1900. President of the Board of Trade 1906-10, Home Secretary 1910-11, First Lord of the Admiralty 1911-15, he resigned after the failure of the Dardanelles expedition, but returned to office as Munitions Minister, War Minister and finally Colonial Secretary under Lloyd George during and after World War One. He was Conservative Chancellor of the Exchequer 1924-1929, but was out of office for most of the 1930s because of his opposition to government attempts to appease Hitler. First Lord of the Admiralty again 1939-1940, he became Prime Minister 1940-45 and was the symbol of British Resistance to Germany. After surprisingly losing the 1945 election, he was Prime Minister again 1951-55, and finally retired as an MP in 1964. He was awarded the Nobel Prize for literature in 1953. His death in the mid-1960s was seen widely as the end of a political era.

FROST David Paradine (born 1939). Educated at

Cambridge, where he was Secretary of the "Footlights", he became a leading television and satire star of the 1960s as anchorman for BBC TV's *That Was the Week That Was* (1962-3). He worked subsequently on numerous other programmes, including *Not So Much a Programme, More a Way of Life* (1964-5), *The Frost Report* (1966-67) and *Frost over England* (1967). Since then he has worked extensively in Britain and the USA; his TV interviewees have included Harold Wilson and President Nixon.

KENNEDY John Fitzgerald (1917-63). Son of diplomat Joseph Kennedy who was American ambassador to Britain 1937-40, he was the successful Democratic candidate in the 1960 Presidential election against Richard Nixon, becoming America's first Roman Catholic President. He was criticized for allowing the disastrous invasion of Cuba by Cuban exiles at the Bay of Pigs (1961), but successfully forced the Russians to remove nuclear weapons from Cuba a year later. He also expanded the American military presence in Vietnam. He was shot dead in Dallas, Texas in November 1963, an event which shocked the world.

MACMILLAN (Maurice) Harold (born 1894). Educated at Eton and Oxford, he fought in World War One and was wounded three times. He was MP for Stockton on Tees 1924-9 and 1931-45, urging 1930s' governments to do more to combat unemployment. He held a series of minor government offices during the Second World War, and was Minister of Housing and Local Government 1951-4, Minister of Defence 1954-5, Foreign Secretary 1955 and Chancellor of the Exchequer 1955-7. As Prime Minister (1957-63), he presided over a period of rapid economic expansion, but an emergency operation forced him to resign in dramatic circumstances in 1963 on the eve of the Conservative Party Conference. A notable writer and TV interviewee, he was created Earl of Stockton in 1984.

NIXON Richard Milhous (born 1913). Republican Vice President of the USA under Eisenhower 1953-61, but narrowly lost the 1960 Presidential election to John F. Kennedy. He retired from politics in 1962 after failing to become governor of California, but made a successful bid for the Presidency in 1968. His first term of office was marked by large-scale American withdrawal from Vietnam, and new links with China after 25 years of hostility. He was re-elected by a huge margin in 1972, but was forced to resign in 1974 (the first American President to do so) after investigations into the "Watergate Affair" revealed widespread government corruption in which he was involved.

POPE PAUL VI (Giovanni Battista Montini, 1897-1978). Cardinal Archbishop of Milan before he was elected Pope in 1963. He was the first Pope to leave Italy in 150 years, and visited the Holy Land, America, India and the Far East. He also sought closer links with communist countries and reassembled the Second Vatican Council begun by his predecessor, John XXIII. He upheld the Church's ban on all artificial methods of birth control in 1968.

QUANT Mary (born 1934). A leading English fashion and cosmetic designer of the 1960s. She founded the Mary Quant group of companies in 1955 and helped to make London the fashion centre of the world with popular lines for the youth market including the mini-skirt. Her rise to fame from comparatively humble origins in South London has led to her being described as one of the products of the "classless" Sixties' society in which a public school education and influential friends were no longer of such importance in advancing your career.

RAMSEY Sir Alfred Ernest (born 1920). International footballer with Southampton and later transferred to Tottenham Hotspur, where he won a League Championship medal in 1951. He played 31 times for England. As manager of Ipswich Town he took the club from the Third Division to the League Championship 1955-63. He was manager of the England team 1963-74, masterminding the winning of the World Cup in 1966 but failing to retain the title in Mexico in 1970. He was knighted in 1967.

RICHARD Cliff (Harry Webb, born 1940). An important British pop idol with eight hits in the 1950s and seven more number ones in the Sixties. Despite the fact that the Sixties was a decade of huge "super groups" and endless new varieties of music, his popularity remained consistent, with such hits as "The Young Ones" (1962), "Bachelor Boy" (1963) and "Congratulations" (1968). He represented Britain in the Eurovision Song Contest twice (1968 and 1973). He became a convert to Evangelical Christianity in 1966.

WHITEHOUSE Mary (born 1910). Teacher, freelance journalist and broadcaster, she was co-founder of the "Clean Up TV campaign" of 1964. As honorary general secretary of the National Viewers and Listeners Association 1965-80 and its president since 1980, she has campaigned tirelessly for less sex and violence on TV and in the mass media. She has published three books: *Who does she think she is?* (1971), *Whatever happened to Sex?* (1977) and *A Most Dangerous Woman?* (1982).

WILSON (James) Harold (born 1916). Educated at Oxford, where he won first class honours in Philosophy, Politics and Economics and became a fellow of University College in 1938. Labour MP for Ormskirk 1945-50 and Huyton 1950-83, he held minor government office 1945-7 and was President of the Board of Trade 1947-51. He was elected leader of the Labour Party on the sudden death of Hugh Gaitskell in 1963, and was Prime Minister 1964-70 and 1974-6, defeating Sir Alec Douglas Home in 1964 and Edward Heath in 1966 and in two elections in 1974. He was created a Baron in 1983.

Difficult Words

Bilateral School	a school which accepts children with a wide range of abilities and offers a wide range of subject choices.
bowl	an alley where ten-pin bowling takes place. A bowl is usually made up of 12 or more "lanes".
BP	British Petroleum – a leading world oil-producing company.
branch line	country railway, usually single-track, joining a main line at a junction.
British Raj	the government system by which Britain ruled India when it was part of the British Empire.
capitalism	economic system in which businesses are privately owned, run for profit and compete against each other.
communism	economic system in which property is held by the state on behalf of all members of society.
Cultural Revolution	period of upheaval in China under Mao Tse-Tung in the 1960s, which led to many communist officials being sacked.
discrimination	giving unfavourable treatment to a group because of differences of race, religion, sex or class.
11+	an exam taken to decide which type of secondary school a child should attend, after age 11.
Flower Power	hippy idea of the 1960s: a strong wish to get back to Nature, and to a simple life of Peace and Love.
latchkey children	children whose parents are out at work all day, and who therefore have to let themselves into the family home when they get back after school.
patriotism	love of one's country and a determination to defend it.
Public School	a school run independently of the state, and which charges fees to its pupils.
ton-up boy	a motorcycle enthusiast, who rides his bike at speeds over the "ton" (100+mph).
TUC	Trades Union Congress – the ruling body of the Trades Union movement.
The Twist	a 1960s' dance, involving violent twisting of the hips.
Vietnam War	war in South-East Asia between local forces backed by America, Russia and China, c. 1950-75.

Book List

Books for Younger Readers

Fab! The Sounds of the Sixties, Tony Jasper, Blandford Press 1984

Growing Up in the 1960s, Richard Tames, Batsford, 1983

For a description of World Events in the 1960s see *The Sixties*, Nathaniel Harris, Macdonald, 1975

Books for Older Readers

Britain since 1945 – A Political History, David Childs, Ernest Benn, 1979

British Society since 1945, Arthur Marwick, Penguin Books, 1982

From Fringe to Flying Circus, Roger Wilmut, Eyre Methuen, 1980

The Neophiliacs, Christopher Booker, William Collins, 1969/Fontana Books, 1970

The Pendulum Years, Bernard Levin, Jonathan Cape Limited, 1970/Pan Books Limited, 1972

Poems of the Sixties, edited by F E S Finn, John Murray, 1970

The Sixties – A Fresh Look at the Decade of Change, Francis Wheen, Century Publishing in association with Channel Four Television Company Limited, 1982

Index